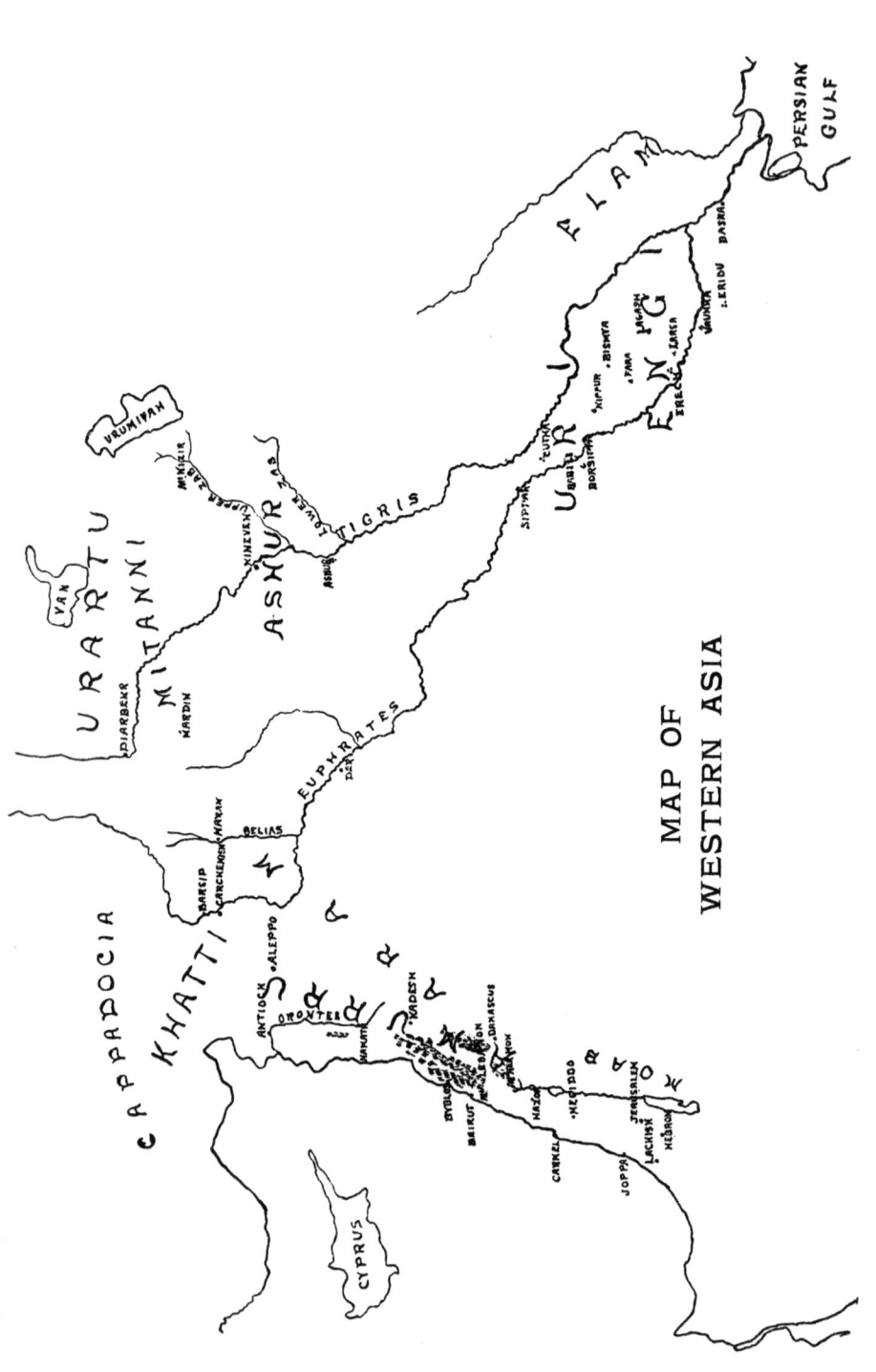

AMURRU

THE HOME OF THE NORTHERN SEMITES

A Study Showing that the Religion and Culture of Israel are Not of Babylonian Origin

BY

ALBERT T. CLAY, Ph.D.

PROFESSOR OF SEMITIC PHILOLOGY AND ARCHÆOLOGY,
UNIVERSITY OF PENNSYLVANIA

WIPF & STOCK · Eugene, Oregon

Wipf and Stock Publishers
199 W 8th Ave, Suite 3
Eugene, OR 97401

Amuru
The Home of the Northern Semites
By Clay, Albert T.
ISBN 13: 978-1-62564-711-5
Publication date 2/24/2014
Previously published by The Sunday School Times Co, 1909

TO
PROFESSOR EDGAR FAHS SMITH
Ph.D. Sc.D. LL.D.
VICE PROVOST OF THE UNIVERSITY OF PENNSYLVANIA

BELOVED BY COLLEAGUES
AND STUDENTS

IN GRATEFUL APPRECIATION

PREFACE

These discussions are the outgrowth of The Reinicker Lectures for the year 1908, delivered at the Protestant Episcopal Theological Seminary, Alexandria, Virginia. Instead of publishing the lectures as delivered, which covered the subject, "Recent Discoveries in Bible Lands," it seemed preferable to present a special phase of the subject, which is here treated more fully than in the lectures.

In the author's work, *Light on the Old Testament from Babel*, a protest was expressed against the claims of the Pan-Babylonists that Babylonia had extensively influenced the culture of Israel. Continued researches have opened up new vistas of the subject, which confirm the contention that the Pan-Babylonists have not only greatly overestimated the influence of the Babylonian culture upon Israel, but that the Semitic Babylonians came from the land of Amurru; that is, Syria and Palestine, and that their culture was an amalgamation of what was once Amorite or West Semitic and the Sumerian which they found in the Euphrates valley.

In order to make the main outlines of the subject as well as the discussions which bear directly upon the Old Testament more readable, the technical material has been confined largely to Part II, but frequent references to it are made in Part I. Instead of quoting the numbers of the pages referred to, they will be found in

6 AMURRU HOME OF NORTHERN SEMITES

the Index. The author realizes that in a number of instances other interpretations of certain individual facts are possible. Modification of views presented must necessarily follow new discoveries as they are made; but nevertheless the writer believes that the main contentions will remain undisturbed.

To my colleagues, Professor J. A. Montgomery and Professor Morris Jastrow, Jr., I am deeply grateful for their generous help and encouragement during the preparation of this book. And I also extend my hearty thanks for the kind assistance rendered by my friends, Professor G. A. Barton, of Bryn Mawr; Professor W. Max Müller, of Philadelphia; Professor Arthur Ungnad, of Jena; the Rev. Dr. C. H. W. Johns, Fellow at Cambridge University; Dr. Hermann Ranke, of Berlin; Dr. Arno Poebel, of Eisenach; and Dr. William Hayes Ward, of New York. To all it gives me pleasure to acknowledge my indebtedness and extend my warm gratitude. Let me add, in mentioning the names of these scholars, that they are in no wise responsible for the views expressed in these lectures.

ALBERT T. CLAY.

UNIVERSITY OF PENNSYLVANIA.

CONTENTS

PART I.
	PAGE
INTRODUCTORY REMARKS	13
CREATION STORY	44
THE SABBATH	55
ANTEDILUVIAN PATRIARCHS	63
DELUGE STORY	71
ORIGINAL HOME OF SEMITIC CULTURE	83

PART II.
AMURRU IN THE CUNEIFORM INSCRIPTIONS	95
AMURRU IN WEST SEMITIC INSCRIPTIONS	150

APPENDIX.
I. UR OF THE CHALDEES	167
II. THE NAME OF JERUSALEM	173
III. THE NAME OF SARGON	181
IV. THE NAME NIN-IB	195
V. THE NAME YAHWEH	202

ABBREVIATIONS

A. D. D.—Johns, *Assyrian Deeds and Documents.*
A. J. S. L.—*American Journal of Semitic Languages.*
A. K. G. W.—*Abhandlungen der philologisch-historischen Classe der Königl. Sächsischen Gesellschaft der Wissenschaften.*
Altbab. Priv.—Meissner, *Beiträge zum Altbabylonischen Privatrecht.*
Asien.—Müller, *Asien und Europa nach Altägyptischen Denkmälern.*
B. A.—*Beiträge zur Assyriologie,* edited by Delitzsch and Haupt.
B. E.—*Babylonian Expedition of the University of Pennsylvania,* Vol. I, 1 and 2, Hilprecht; VI, 1, Ranke; VI, 2, Poebel; VIII, 1, Clay; IX, Hilprecht and Clay; X, Clay; XIV, Clay; XV, Clay; and XX, Hilprecht.
Babyloniaca.—Edited by Virolleaud.
Bezold, *Catalogue.*—*Catalogue of the Cuneiform Tablets in the Kouyunjik Collection.*
Brown, *Heb. Dic.*—Brown, Driver and Briggs, *Hebrew and English Lexicon of the Old Testament.*
Brünnow, *List*—*A Classified List of Cuneiform Ideographs.*
C. T.—*Cuneiform Texts from Babylonian Tablets, etc., in the British Museum,* by King, Pinches and Thompson.
Découvertes—de Sarzec Heuzey, *Décourvertes en Chaldée.*
Dél. en Perse—Scheil, *Textes Elamites Sémitiques, Délégation en Perse.*
Ephemeris—Lidzbarski, *Ephemeris für Semitische Epigraphik.*
J. B. L.—*Journal of Biblical Literature.*
J. R. A. S.—*Journal of the Royal Asiatic Society.*
Harper, *Letters*—*Assyrian and Babylonian Letters,* Vols. I to VII.
H. W. B.—Delitzsch, *Assyrian Handwörterbuch.*
Huber, *Personennamen*—*Die Personennamen in der Keilschrifturkunden aus der Zeit der Könige von Ur und Nisin.*
Jastrow, *Rel.*—*Die Religion Babyloniens und Assyriens.*
K.—*Kouyunjik Collection in Bezold's Catalogue of the British Museum.*
K. A. T.[3]—*Die Keilinschriften und das Alte Testament,* by Zimmern and Winckler.

K. B.—*Keilinschriftliche Bibliothek.*
King, *Chronicles*—*Chronicles Concerning Early Babylonian Kings,* Vols. I and II.
Meissner, *Ideogr.*—*Seltene Assyrische Ideogramme.*
Meissner, *Supplement*—*Supplement zu den Assyrischen Wörterbüchern.*
Muss-Arnolt, *Dict.*—*Concise Dictionary of the Assyrian Languages.*
Nöldeke, *Festschrift*—*Orientalische Studien Theodor Nöldeke zum siebzigsten Geburtstag.*
O. L. Z.—*Orientalistische Literatur-Zeitung,* edited by Peiser.
Prolegomena—Delitzsch, *Prolegomena eines neuen Hebräisch-Aramäischen Wörterbuch zum Alten Testament.*
P. S. B. A.—*Proceedings of the Society of Biblical Archæology.*
Ranke, P. N.—*Early Babylonian Personal Names,* B. E., D, Vol. III.
R., I., etc., or Rawlinson—*The Cuneiform Inscriptions of Western Asia,* Vols. I to V.
Rev. Ass.—*Revue d'Assyriologie.*
R. S.—*Revue Sémitique.*
Rec. Tab. Chal.—Thureau-Dangin, *Recueil de Tablettes Chaldéennes.*
Strassmaier, *Nbk., Nbn.,* etc.—*Babylonische Texte, Inschriften von Nabuchodonosor.*
Tallqvist, *Namenbuch*—*Neubabylonisches Namenbuch zu den Geschäftsurkunden.*
V. B.—Thureau-Dangin, *Die Sumerischen und Akkadischen Königsinschriften*—*Vorderasiatische Bibliothek,* I, Ab. 1.
V. S.—*Vorderasiatische Schriftdenkmäler,* Vols. III, VII, etc., Ungnad.
Z. A., or *Zeit. für Ass.*—*Zeitschrift für Assyriologie,* edited by Bezold.
Z. A. T. W.—*Zeitschrift für die alttestamentliche Wissenschaft,*—
Z. D. M. G.—*Zeitschrift der Deutschen Morgenländischen Gesellschaft.*

PART I

INTRODUCTORY REMARKS

THE current theory of Semitic scholars concerning the origin of the Semitic Babylonians is that they came from Arabia, and that after their culture had developed in Babylonia it was carried westward into *Amurru* (*i.e.*, Palestine and Syria[1]) generally known as the land of the Amorites.

Without attempting to determine the ultimate origin of the Semites, the writer holds that every indication, resulting from his investigations, proves that the movement of the Semites was eastward from Amurru and Aram (*i.e.*, from the lands of the West) into Babylonia. In other words, the culture of the Semitic Babylonians points, if not to its origin, at least to a long development in Amurru before it was carried into Babylonia.

As a matter of fact, the earliest name for Northern Babylonia in the inscriptions is *Ûri*. Shumer or Southern Babylonia, was called *Engi*, and Northern Babylonia was called *Ûri*; *i.e.*, Babylonia, as well as the district extending to the shore of the Mediterranean, was called *Ûri* or *Âri*. The name *Ûri* or *Âri*, it will be shown, is very probably derived from *Amurru*, the name of the West country. This shows that the name of Baby-

---

[1] See Barton, *Semitic Origins*, chap. I, and Paton, *Early History of Palestine and Syria*, chaps. III–VIII.

14 AMURRU HOME OF NORTHERN SEMITES

lonia, which is *Uri* in the earliest known period of Semitic Babylonian history, is a geographical extension of the land in the West, known as *Amurru* or *Uri*. Not only was the name of the country *Amurru* carried to that region, but it will also be demonstrated that the culture of the Semitic Babylonians was largely transported from the West. The Amorites in moving eastward into Babylonia carried with them not only their religion, but their traditions, such as their creation story, antediluvian patriarchs, deluge legend, etc. In considering the position taken by the Pan-Babylonists in Part I, concerning these and other subjects, the above statements, which are fully discussed in Part II, should be kept constantly in mind.

A little more than a decade ago there appeared in Germany a school of critics known generally as the Pan-Babylonian or Astral-mythological School. The parallels to certain features of the Bible stories that are found in the Babylonian literature determined for the Pan-Babylonists that the origin of much of the Hebrew culture is to be found in Babylonian mythology. The work of Stucken, *Astralmythen*, Part I, on Abraham, published in 1896, which was followed by Part II, on Lot, in 1897, may be said to be the beginning of these efforts; although similar conceptions of the Old Testament antedate this work.

Professor Winckler, of Berlin, may be said to be the real founder of the school. In a series of contributions from his pen, following his *Geschichte Israels*, Vol. II, which was published in 1900, he has unfolded his theory of the Universe. The world consists of heaven and earth. The heavens are subdivided into the northern heavens, the zodiac, and the heavenly ocean. The earthly part of the universe also consists of a threefold division, the heaven, the earth, and the waters beneath the earth. In this system the signs of the zodiac play the important part, for the planets as they passed through the heavens enabled the astrologers to interpret the will of their deities. Upon these ideas a complete cosmological system is worked out. The heavens, corresponding to the earth, reflect their influence upon it, with the result that everything in heaven has its counterpart on earth. The gods of heaven have dwellings on earth, presided over by earthly kings, who as representatives of the gods are considered their incarnations. The heavens reveal the past, present, and the future for those who could read them. What occurs on earth is only a copy of what occurred in heaven. Astrology, therefore, was the all-important test and interpreter of ancient history. All ancient nations, including Israel, practised it or were influenced by it.

The periodic changes in the positions of the heavenly bodies gave rise to certain sacred numbers. These Winckler uses to show the bearing of the Babylonian astral mythology upon things Israelitish. According to his views, not only is the Israelitish cult dependent upon Babylonian originals, but also the patriarchs and other leaders of Israel, such as Joshua, Gideon, Saul, David, and others, are sun or lunar mythological personages.

Abraham and Lot are the same as the *Gemini*, called by the Romans Castor and Pollux. Abraham, together with his wife, who was also his sister, are forms of *Tammuz* (who was a solar god) and *Ishtar*, the former being the brother and bridegroom of the latter. As *Ishtar* was the daughter of *Sin*, the moon-god, Abraham must be a moon-god; for he went from Ur to Haran, two places dedicated to that deity. Many circumstances of the myths concerning Abraham corroborate this. The 318 men who were Abraham's allies, in the fourteenth chapter of Genesis, are the 318 days of the year when the moon is visible. All Babylonian gods were represented by numbers. Kirjath-arba, the one center of Abraham myths, means the "city of Arba, or four." *Arba* must then be the moon-god which has four phases. Beersheba, "the seven wells," another center with which Abraham myths were identified, also represents the moon, because there are seven days in each phase of the moon. Isaac, who lived at Beersheba, must, therefore, also be a moon deity. The four wives of Jacob show that he also is the same. His twelve sons are the twelve months. Leah's seven sons are the gods of the week. The twelve hundred pieces of silver which Benjamin received represent a multiple of the thirty days of the month; and the five changes of garments that he received are the five intercalary days of the Babylonian year.

In Joseph, Winckler sees a *Tammuz*, or sun-myth. His dream shows the priority of the sun. Esau identified with Edom is the same, as is shown by his "redness." The stories of Moses, Joshua (who is another form of Moses), Ehud, Gideon, are sun-myths. In David, Winckler finds more evidence of a solar origin than in all other biblical characters. Solomon and others are explained as having the same origin. The recurrence of characteristic numbers is the chief criterion by which these supposed facts are determined.

Professor Zimmern, of Leipzig,[1] also belongs to this school, but pays more attention to analogies, and to the dependence of the Hebrew stories upon Babylonian originals, than to the recurrence of numbers. Features of the Old Testament stories that are parallel to certain features in the Babylonian literature point, he believes, unmistakably to Babylonian origin. The incorporation of the Babylonian creation story in the Old Testament shows that in Israel the writer considered Yahweh to be identical with Marduk. Later, these same elements of the Marduk cult were applied to Christ by the Christian Jews. The story of the birth of Christ has its origin in the fabled birth of Marduk. Babylonian elements are also found in the regal office of Christ, as well as in His passion. Ashurbanipal, as a "penitent expiator," gave rise to the story of His weeping over Jerusalem and His agony in the garden. His death is suggested by that of Marduk and Tammuz; and the idea of His descent into Hades comes from the goddess Ishtar's descent. The resurrection is a repetition of Marduk and Tammuz myths, etc.[2]

---

[1] See *Keilinschrifttexten und das Alte Testament*.

[2] For a fuller statement of the views of Winckler and Zimmern, see Barton, *Biblical World*, 1908, pp. 436 ff.

Dr. Alfred Jeremias, of Leipzig, by his publication, *Das Alte Testament im Lichte des alten Orients,* has popularized the views of this school, but fortunately makes his position more reasonable by admitting the possibility that the patriarchs may be historical personages; for example, the twelve sons of Jacob, he says, represent the zodiacal signs, and yet it is possible that they may be historical persons.

Professor Jensen, of Marburg, in a work published in 1906, of over a thousand pages, *Das Gilgamesch-Epos in der Weltliteratur,* finds the origin of the biblical characters of Abraham down to Christ, including John the Baptist, in this Babylonian collection of sun-myths. The Gospels he calls "Mythographs." Even references to biblical characters in the ancient monuments are explained away, or no account is taken of them. In short, the origin of what we know as Israelitish is really an adaptation by late Hebrew writers of the Babylonian sun-myths, which had been woven together into what is known as the Gilgamesh epic.

In one of the pamphlets issued this year by Jensen, entitled *Moses Jesus Paulus,* he defends his views against his critics. His position is stated in the words: "The old Israelitish history, the history of Jesus of Nazareth, has collapsed, and the apostolic history has been exploded. Babylon has laid Babylon in ruins—a catastrophe for the Old and New Testament science, but truly not undeserved; a catastrophe for the mythology of our church and synagogue, which reaches into our present time like a beautiful ruin."

INTRODUCTORY REMARKS 19

By the expression, "Babylon has laid Babylon in ruins," Prof. Jensen evidently means that the discoveries which have been used to establish the historical value of the Old Testament are now used to show that the foundations upon which the Christian and Jewish theology rest are borrowed from Babylonian mythology. The same phrase in question is, however, equally applicable in these lectures, for the claim is that Babylonian researches show that the contentions of the Pan-Babylonists are without foundation, and that the literature of Israel is not to be regarded as being composed of transformed Babylonian and Assyrian myths.

Some of these scholars and their followers hold that only a change of names has taken place. On the one hand, all that originally belonged to Marduk is transferred to Christ; and on the other, the legends of Gilgamesh have been adopted and adapted by the Hebrews, so that all which refers to the life of Christ—his passion, his death, his descent, his resurrection and his ascension—are to be explained as having their origin in Babylonian mythology.

Although these theories have been advanced by some of the foremost scholars, they need more proof before they can be seriously considered as more than conjectures similar to those that have been based on Greek and Roman mythology for centuries. The anthropomorphic character of the gods enables one to find parallels, in one form or another, for practically everything that took place in the lives of all biblical characters, even in that of the Nazarene. For example, in Greek mythology, Tammuz, the darling of Aphrodite, was slain; but on the third day they rejoiced at the resurrection of this lord of light—who also was known by the name of *Iaw*. A more striking parallel could not be desired. Further, this name *Iaw* has rightly been said to represent closely the divine name Yahweh, as it appears in the inscriptions; hence additional far-reaching conjectures could be offered. As a matter of fact, Greek mythology offers far more interesting parallels than the Babylonian.

The German savants who belong to this school have their counterparts in England and on this side of the Atlantic. The celestial light has penetrated these shores and we have seen in the past and are beginning to see more and more the reflections flare up in a modified as well as in an intensified form.

The dependence of the culture of Israel upon Babylonia seems to be conceded by almost every scholar. This conception has grown steadily within the last few decades, so that the edifice which has been reared has now reached its full height, the capstone has been set, and the structure is complete. A change of names, that is all, and a Babylonian deity, Marduk or Bel, becomes Christ.

The writer feels that the very height to which this creation has attained is the salutary feature of the whole effort, for the foundation upon which it rests is of such a character that it will surely cause the entire structure to fall. It is not the purpose of this discussion to take down one stone after another and submit them

INTRODUCTORY REMARKS 21

to an examination, and so endeavor to reduce the height and keep the building within proper proportions; but it is the purpose to examine carefully the very foundation stones of the structure and ascertain upon what it rests.

Before discussing some of the important claims of these critics, a word may be said with reference to the Babylonian astral ideas and Israel. In the first place, contrary to the position taken by Winckler and his school that astronomy took its rise in the early period of Babylonian history, it is now maintained by Kugler,[1] Jastrow,[2] and others, that the period when the science of astronomy was developed in Babylonia was between the fourth and second centuries B.C., that is to say, during the period of Greek influence in the Euphrates Valley. Kugler[3] dates the earliest astronomical tablet 522 B.C., although he admits that it shows evidence of being revised from an earlier tablet. While an argument *e silentio* is precarious, this absence of astronomical inscriptions of the character that is supposed to have influenced Israel is strikingly significant.

More important is the fact that there is absolutely no proof for the existence of such an astral conception of the universe in the Old Testament. In fact, as far as is known to the writer, there is an utter lack of data

---

[1] *Kulturhistorische Bedeutung der Babylonischen Astronomie*, p. 38 ff.
[2] *Proceedings of the American Philosophical Society*, XLVII, No. 190, 1908, p. 667.
[3] *Sternkunde und Sterndienst in Babel*, I, p. 2.

upon which these astral theories rest.¹ Surely the injunction to have nothing to do with astrology cannot be construed as countenancing it. In Deuteronomy 12 : 2–7, the law required that the man who worshiped the sun, moon, or any of the host of heaven, should be put to death. The same spirit is maintained in Deuteronomy 4 : 15, 19. See also in what contempt and ridicule the prophet (Is. 47 : 13) spoke of the astrologers, star-gazers, and monthly prognosticators, when he tells the people to let these save them from the coming disasters. That the people of Canaan, or rather of Amurru, worshiped the sun, moon and stars, and perhaps divined by them, seems to be evident from these injunctions; but the legislation against astrology in Israel surely is sufficient proof that it had not penetrated the cult, even if some of the people were influenced by it.

The same is true of liver divination, which serves as another illustration of Israel's attitude towards such practises. The requirement of the Mosaic law to destroy the so-called "caul" above the liver is a proof that in Israel divination by the liver was not sanctioned. We know that the Babylonians believed that by inspecting the liver of the sheep they could ascertain what the gods desired to communicate to them. Through the researches of Professor Jastrow,[2] we have obtained an excellent understanding of this practise of the Babylonians. The Greeks, Romans, and

---

[1] See Rogers, *Religion of Babylonia and Assyria*, p. 220.
[2] See his *Religion Babyloniens und Assyriens*, II, p. 174 ff.

Etruscans also divined by the liver. To what extent the peoples of Amurru practised hepatoscopy is not known. But in the Pentateuch, in no less than ten passages a protest is implied against this kind of divination.[1] The ordinance provides for the burning of the "caul above the liver," which Professor Moore has shown refers to the finger-shaped appendix of the caudate lobe, although the rest of the liver was permitted to be eaten. The reason they were required to burn this part of the liver, as Professor Jastrow has suggested, is that it was a symbolical protest against the use of the liver for divination purposes. By destroying this portion, which played such an important part in hepatoscopy, the people were warned not to divert the sacrifice into a form of divination. We reach, therefore, the same conclusion. The cult, while recognizing the existence of such practises, cannot be said to be even tainted with them; but by its protests emphasizes the importance of holding aloof from them. And, at the same time, it cannot be said that these regulations were directed especially against Babylonian influences; because astrology and liver divination appear to have been widespread in antiquity, and doubtless were in vogue among other peoples beside those already mentioned—in all probability among the Canaanite nations.

Many theories of these and other scholars have arisen and have found acceptance, on the supposition that there is no antiquity for the Hebrew culture as early

---

[1] See Ex. 29 : 13, 22; Lev. 3 : 4, 10, 15; 7 : 4; 8 : 16, 25; 9 : 10, 19.

24 AMURRU HOME OF NORTHERN SEMITES

as Abraham's time. The ancestors of the Hebrews are considered by many of these writers to be nomadic Arabs who came up from Arabia about the time of Abraham; not because one iota of evidence has been produced to discredit the accounts concerning the origin of the Hebrews, as preserved in the Old Testament, namely, that they came from Aram (or Aram-Naharaim), but simply because the speculations of these scholars have led them to such conclusions. And yet, contrary to what has been claimed, many discoveries that have been made in the past decades of research and investigation tend to show the historical value of these relics of antiquity.

Let us inquire what the excavations have thus far revealed concerning this interpenetration of the Babylonian culture in Israel. During the past years explorations have been conducted principally at four sites in Palestine belonging to the early period, namely, Lachish and Gezer in the South, and Ta'annek and Megiddo in the North. On first impressions these excavations might serve the Pan-Babylonists better than anything else with arguments for the mythological character of the entire history of Israel. If we did not know that Israel actually lived in Palestine, we would scarcely have inferred it from what these excavations have revealed. However, according to the recent report of Macalister, an interesting old Hebrew calendar inscription has been found at Gezer. Macalister placed the date of it in the sixth century B.C., but Lidzbarski thinks it is the oldest, or at all events one of the oldest, of West Semitic inscriptions.[1] Unfortunately, systematic excavations in Amurru proper, *i.e.*, the Lebanon district, have not yet been conducted. This deprives us of the proper tests for this thesis.

The lack of archæological remains is due to two important facts. Israel used a perishable material for ordinary writing purposes; and the nation, like other pure Semitic peoples, while possessing a literature, apparently did not develop the plastic arts. We need not expect to find great creations in sculpture and architecture by the Hebrews or, in fact, by any other pure Semitic people of ancient times. The antiquities of artistic value found in Babylonia were in all probability produced by foreigners, perhaps the Sumerians, who belonged to a non-Semitic race. While some work discovered in Assyria is of a comparatively high order, especially in the depicting of animals, we must bear in mind that the black-headed Sumerian was still extant in that land. When Israel was ready to build the temple, Phœnician artificers were secured. While the Phœnicians spoke a Semitic tongue, their art, which is generally acknowledged to be hybrid Egyptian, may indicate also a mixture in race. The works of art accredited to them would be sufficient proof for this conjecture. In short, the archæological remains discovered in Palestine are of such a character that, up to the present time, there is little to show that Israel developed an art—yes, even to show that such a people actually occupied the land.

---

[1] See *Palestine Exploration Fund*, January, 1909, p. 26.

This much can be emphasized, without taking into consideration the clay tablets found in that district which will be discussed later: the excavations conducted in Palestine do not show any Babylonian influence in the early period of Israelitish history, nor in the pre-Israelitish. In the late Assyrian period, when the armies of that nation again and again overran the land, when Assyrian officials in many cases were set over cities and put into control of affairs, it is perfectly natural that traces of the Assyrians should be discovered; especially when we know that towns were repeopled with Assyrians after the natives were carried into exile. While proofs depending upon antiquities discovered up to the present which show such an occupation are exceedingly slight, it is perfectly proper to expect, if certain cities are excavated, to hear at any time of the finding of many importations from Assyria, such as arms, utensils, seals, etc. But, as stated above, these will be found to belong to the time when Assyria was the dominant power in Western Asia.

After surveying the results of the excavations conducted in Palestine we must, therefore, agree with Nowack, who in his review[1] of the work of Schumacher and Steuernagel at Tel el-Mutesselim (1908), takes issue with those who claim predominant influence of Babylonian culture in Palestine from the third millennium on. He says: "It is a disturbing but irrefutable fact that until down to the fifth stratum—*i.e.*, to the

---

[1] *Theol. Literaturzeitung*, 1908, No. 26.

INTRODUCTORY REMARKS 27

beginning of the eighth century—important Assyrian influences do not assert themselves." "It is most significant that in Megiddo not a single idol (*Gottesbild*) from the Assyrian-Babylonian Pantheon has been found." "Some proofs of Assyrian-Babylonian influence are first met in the fifth and sixth stratum; while this is limited, so far as I can see, to the seals found there."[1]

On the other hand, the relations with Egypt are shown by the antiquities discovered to have existed as early as the twelfth dynasty; and much evidence has been secured to prove that the Semites in Canaan were strongly influenced from that quarter. This is not surprising because of the proximity of Egypt, and, as regards Israel, because the Hebrews for centuries lived in that land; but it fails to substantiate the completely Babylonian nature of Canaanitish civilization in the centuries before the Exodus, or in fact at any other time.

This predominance of Egyptian influence as against the Babylonian is well established in the art as represented upon the seal cylinders coming from this district. Sellin's excavations at Tell Ta'annek show that the Palestinians imported seal cylinders from Babylonia, but engraved upon them Egyptian hieroglyphic symbols. In the seals which came from Phœnicia, including Palestine and the Hauran—in other words, the Amorite land, or

---

[1] See Vincent, *Canaan d'après l'exploration récente*, pp. 341, 439, and Cooke, *The Religion of Ancient Palestine*, p. 112 f.

the land called Amurru in these discussions—the Egyptian influence is predominant as early as the third millennium B.C. Such elements as the Egyptian hawk, apron, *crux ansata*, papyrus flower, lion sphynx, vulture, etc., are much in evidence.[1]

As set forth in Part II, on *Amurru in the West Semitic Inscriptions*, the excavations by Macalister and others in Palestine point to the fact that the dominant people in the Westland, whom we call Amorites, in the millennium preceding the time of Moses, were Semites; and further, as shown in Part II, on *Amurru in the Cuneiform Inscriptions*, there are evidences which determine that in the earliest known historical period the Amorite culture was already fully developed, and that it played an important rôle in influencing other peoples. Very appropriately, therefore, inquiry should be made whether the Egyptian inscriptions throw any light upon the question. Do they show that there was a culture in that land in the early period? If so, was it a Semitic culture? And finally, are there any evidences that this culture influenced other peoples?

'*A-ma-ra* or '*A-mu-ra* in the Egyptian inscriptions is known as a geographical term, and refers to the Lebanon region. It may even include the coast, being a vague term for central Syria. The race of the Amorites, according to the Egyptian pictures, is Semitic, and in no

---

[1] See Ward, *Cylinders and other Ancient Seals in the Library of J. Pierpont Morgan*, p. 89.

way distinguished from the other inhabitants of southern and middle Syria.[1]

The monuments of Egypt not only furnish ample evidence to prove that the civilization of Syria-Palestine is Semitic, and is as old as that of Egypt,[2] but, on the authority of Prof. W. M. Müller, it may be stated that the beginnings of civilization in the Nile valley seem to have been extensively influenced by the Western Semites. Contrary to the views of most Semitists, who have followed the writer of the Egyptian "Prunkinschriften," which misrepresents the Asiatics by describing them as miserable, hungry, dirty "sand wanderers," or the *Sinuhe* novel, which endeavors to give the impression that the people of Palestine were in a state of barbarism 2000 B.C., Prof. Müller maintains that in the districts of arable land the people were agricultural, and had attained a fair degree of civilization. The Egyptian pictures of the nomadic or half nomadic traders and mercenaries coming to Egypt at that time show their skill in metal working and weaving. Remarkable weapons and handsomely decorated garments are depicted.

---

[1] This I learn on the authority of Prof. W. M. Müller. The comparison made by Prof. Sayce, *Patriarchal Palestine*, p. 48, with the Libyan type (which strongly resembles the Semitic type) was based on a rather poor picture of "the prince of '*A-ma-ra*" (*L. D.*, 209, or Rosellini, *Mon. Stor.*, p. 143, etc.; also Petrie, *Racial Types*). Better pictures of the Amorites, who are always represented as Semites, are to be found in Sethos I attacking "the land of Qadesh of the land of Amar" (Rosellini, *Mon. Stor.*, p. 53; or Champollion, *Monuments*, p. 295); and also the picture of the prince of that city in W. M. Müller, *Egyptol. Researches*, II, pl. 7.

[2] See Müller, *Orien. Lit. Zeit.*, XI, p. 403.

Already at this time a papyrus speaks of Pharaoh's messengers going to Syria with inscribed bricks tied in their loin cloths.[1] This gives us an earlier date for the use of the cuneiform script in Egypt and Western Asia. Pharaoh Pepy, about 2500 B.C., describes his Asiatic enemies as largely agricultural, and living in strongly fortified cities. It would seem that some of the walls of their cities were no less than fifty feet high.[2] The adoption of Syrian loan words shows powerful influence exercised by the Semites on Egypt before 3000 B.C.[2] Even prior to Menes this Semitic civilization played an important part in the development of Egyptian culture. Prof. Müller further informs me that, according to linguistic and racial indications, in the earliest time no other than the Semite appears to have lived in the Amurru region, where he became sedentary and agricultural as early as the Egyptian in the Nile valley.[3]

In this connection a word is appropriate with reference to the influence of Babylonian and Sumerian civilization upon Egypt. There is little doubt that the Sumerian culture will eventually be shown to have existed at a much earlier date than thus far ascertained by the excavations in Babylonia. But to call Egyptian civilization a branch of the Babylonian, or Sumerian, seems to be a statement without support. Contrary to the claims of Prof. Hommel, although it is quite likely

---

[1] See Müller, *Orien. Lit. Zeit.*, IV, p. 8.
[2] Petrie, *Deshasheh*, pl. 4, represents an Asiatic city stormed by Egyptians in the 5th dynasty.
[3] See Müller, *Orien. Lit. Zeit.*, X, p. 403.

that the beginnings of Egyptian civilization were brought from Asia, not a single Sumerian loan word has been shown to exist in Egyptian, and yet the Sumerian continued in use as late as 2000 B.C., and the Babylonian language was extensively a mixture of the Sumerian and the Semitic. The elements of culture that migrated from Babylonia or Shumer to Egypt must have first been adopted by the Semitic inhabitants of Syria, and transmitted by them. Naturally, this forces us to regard the barbarous Syrian of this early age in another light. And it also forces us to realize that the references to Amurru in the oldest cuneiform inscriptions are indications of the correctness of the contentions for the early civilization of that land. In short, all this attests the credibility of the claims made on the basis of the Palestinian excavations and other researches, that an ancient Semitic people, with a not inconsiderable civilization, lived in Amurru prior to the time of Abraham.

It is well known that Babylonian and Sumerian rulers in the earliest known historical period—that is, in the third and fourth millenniums before Christ—conquered and held in subjection the land of Syria and Palestine. In this period Gudea is found importing limestone, alabaster, cedars, etc., from the West, even gold from the Sinaitic peninsula. A succession of Babylonian rulers claimed suzerainty over this land until it fell into the hands of Elam. With the overthrow of that land, Amurru (Palestine and Syria) came again into the possession of Babylonia in Hammurabi's time. Later, during the eighteenth dynasty of Egypt, it is found in the control of the Pharaohs.

32 AMURRU HOME OF NORTHERN SEMITES

The military conquest and enforced subjection of the country for such a long period resulted in the establishment of the Babylonian language and script as the official tongue of the entire district controlled, as well as of other parts of Western Asia and Egypt. The ability to master this complicated and difficult system of writing, many have thought, speaks volumes for the intelligence of the civilized peoples of Western Asia. Education of scribes must have been widely spread; for the learned knew how to write this cumbersome ideographic and phonetic script of the Babylonians. We find the Hittite. the Mitannæan, the Egyptian, the Amorite, and other peoples using it; but the Hebrews, who have handed down a literature of a very high order, purporting to deal with and to come from this period,[1] we are informed by critics, were uncivilized or semi-barbarous nomads; not that any evidences of an archæological or any other character have been produced in substantiation of this view, but simply because their theories demand such conclusions.

Perhaps the most important argument used by scholars to show the influence of Babylonia upon Canaan has been the fact that among the tablets discovered at Tel el-Amarna, in Egypt, two Babylonian epics were recovered. This fact also furnished a definite time when the supposed Babylonian influence was exerted upon Canaan. One of these myths contains

---

[1] The writer is one of the small minority who believes that Hebraic (or Amoraic) literature, as well as Aramaic, has a great antiquity prior to the first millennium B.C.

what is known as the *Adapa* legend, and the other refers to *Ereshkigal*, the consort of the god *Nergal*, and her messenger *Namtar*. These, as has been inferred, were used as text-books in learning the language, as is shown by the fact that they were interpunctuated, the words being separated by marks made with ink, in order to facilitate their study.

It seems the finding of these so-called Babylonian myths in Egypt offers no better proof for the influence of Babylonian ideas upon the cults of the West than the discovery of text-books in French at the present time upon one of the islands of the Pacific would show influence from France upon the cult of the inhabitants. It would, knowing certain facts, show that both languages were used for diplomatic and social intercourse between nations; the former in the second millennium before Christ, and the latter in the nineteenth and twentieth centuries of the Christian era; but until it can be shown that the people of the Western lands actually adopted or assimilated Babylonian myths or religious ideas (many of which the writer holds are Western), no such far-reaching conclusions, based upon the theory that when Israel entered Canaan all these Babylonian ideas were a part of the mental possession of the people, can be maintained. Discoveries in Egypt, Phœnicia, or any other nation of the West do not show traces of this influence. These nations had cults of their own, showing a long history of development, prior to the Amarna period. Moreover, Israel, entering Canaan about that time, surely was not in a position and in a frame of mind to select from the older and current beliefs what should constitute her faith. The cult of the Israelites grew up under unconscious influences quietly at work during the generations which preceded, reaching far back into the ages. It is, however, quite reasonable to suppose that the culture of Canaan had more or less influence in one way or another upon Israel. It is not improbable also that the Kenites with whom Moses sojourned, and with whom Israel came into contact, influenced the Hebrew cult, but to what extent can be determined only when we know more about their civilizations.

Naturally, if it is assumed that the Babylonians were the only people who had a religion in that era in Western Asia, the theory would appear more reasonable. But, of course, this cannot be maintained. Philology and archæology have extended our horizon, so that our conception of the civilizations of that age is that they were of a highly developed character. With the Amorites and Aramæans in the North, the Egyptians and Arabians in the South, as well as the old Amorite culture in the land which they occupied, it seems unreasonable to assume such a wholesale dependence upon far-off Babylonian culture, simply because in certain periods Amurru was under the control of Babylon, or because certain literature, some of which is Western, has been preserved for us by reason of the fact that it was written upon clay, whereas most of the other nations wrote on perishable material; and also because two practically indestructible tablets containing so-called Babylonian myths happened to have been found in Egypt. On the contrary, as the discussion proceeds, we shall see how Babylonia was invaded by West Semitic peoples who carried their culture thither.

It must be acknowledged that the Hebrew, during the many ages of his history, has been peculiarly subject to the influences of his environment. A notable characteristic of the race is the adaptability of the people to their surroundings. But here we should also recall that Herodotus said that the Persians more easily than others adopted foreign customs. The influence of Babylonia upon the habits and life of Israel after the exile is well recognized. But even this is greatly overestimated, for many things that are actually Aramæan have been regarded as Babylonian. Persian and Hellenic influences also are recognized. We must not fail to remember, however, that during these periods the nation was disorganized. But still, in the pre-exilic period we have only to read the prophets and the codes, to see how susceptible Israel apparently was to the influences at work about them, and how prone the people were to wander.

We also learn that the high standard required by the codes was in many points not realized, so that precept and practise were widely separated. There seems to have taken place, in many instances, what may properly be called an accommodation to the actual practises of the people, which crept into Israel in spite of the efforts of the leaders to keep them out. Moreover, it would be unfair to the ancient lawgiver, and to the leaders of Israel, if we acknowledged that the cult itself was even subject to modification as the people became acquainted with or were influenced by the practises of their environment.

Gunkel holds that "as long as the Israelitic religion was in its vigor it assimilated actively this foreign material; in later times, when the religion had become relaxed in strength, it swallowed foreign elements, feathers and all." If this statement of the readiness of Israel to assimilate, in such a wholesale manner, the ideas of foreign peoples depends upon what has been shown to have been actually assimilated in the late period, the verdict must be, it rests upon weak premises.

That Delitzsch, in his *Babel und Bibel* lectures, "is right in calling Canaan at the time of the Exodus a domain of Babylonian culture," is a statement most difficult to understand in the light of the known facts. If it were true, should we not expect the chief deity of the Babylonians to figure prominently in the West? If the influence of the Babylonian religion upon the West were as great as is asserted by scholars, should we not expect to find in the early literature of that land, for instance, the name of *Marduk*, who for half a millennium prior to the Exodus had been the head of the Babylonian pantheon? This name was used extensively in the nomenclature,—the name above all names, the god that had absorbed the attributes and prerogatives of all other gods. Surely, if the influence was so extensive upon the West, we ought to find the name Marduk figuring prominently in the

Amarna letters, in the Ta'annek inscriptions, in the Cappadocian tablets published by Delitzsch, Sayce, and Pinches, and in the portions of the Old Testament belonging to the early period. But, with one exception in the Amarna letters, where is the name? The argument *e silentio* is unscientific, but this silence at least is most significant. And where is the epithet of *Marduk*, namely, *Bêl*, which was taken from *Ellil*? According to the revision of the Amarna texts by Knudtzon, the only occurrence is the questionable [*B*]*e*-[*e*]*l*-[*sh*]*a*-*a*[*m*]-*m*[*a*], every character of which is in doubt. And where is the name *Ellil* in these letters,[1] from whom the title *Bêl* was taken, except in the name of *Kadashman-Ellil*, the Babylonian ruler? *Ellil* is the lord of lands, to whom the rulers of the country, ancient as well as modern, did obeisance at the great Nippurian sanctuary, and whose name figures so prominently as an element in personal names. Why, it can properly be asked, is the mention of this deity (who was considered by the Assyrians to be the god *par excellence* of the Babylonians) not found in Palestine? In the inscriptions of the Cassite period, *Nusku* is a most important deity in the nomenclature. At Nippur the name of *Nusku*, together with that of *Ellil* and *NIN-IB*, is used in the oath formula; but where is this deity found in the literature of Canaan of this period? The same is true of *Nergal*, the god of Cutha, with the exceptions of the Babylonian myth found in Egypt. Nergal's name in

---

[1] A certain *Ellil-bâni* occurs in the Cappadocian tablets published by Sayce, and by Pinches.

the Cassite period is also extensively used in the nomenclature.¹ In a tablet found at Tell el-Amarna from *Alashia*, which is supposed to be Cyprus, a god *MASH-MASH* occurs, which has been read *Nergal*, but for which a better reading would be *LUGAL Urra*, "King Uru," which is equivalent to Nergal, but which is one of the names in the inscriptions for the great solar deity of the West (see Part II). And where is *NIN-LIL* or *Nanâ* or *Bau* or *GU-LA* or any other form of the goddess Ishtar found? Only in the letters from Mitanni, which is north of and in proximity to Assyria, does the name Ishtar occur. Instead, we find *Ashirta* or *Ashrati*, which is the name of the goddess indigenous to the land.

Among the deities in the Amarna letters, the Babylonian writing *IB* and *NIN-IB* are found; but, as we shall see in Part II, these are cuneiform signs which probably stood for the West Semitic *Eshu* and the *Ba'al* of Amurru or *Mâshu*. In other words, they represent deities or epithets of the solar god or gods of the land in which the letters were written, namely, Amurru. *Shamash, Adad, Ûru, Dagan,* etc., are also found, but, as we shall see, the West is their proper habitat. In Part II it will be shown that Marduk, Nergal, and other deities are Amoritish. Then an explanation why these names are not found in the early literature of the West is in order. As we shall see in Part II, while they are West Semitic, they represent originally only

---

¹ See Clay, *B. E.*, XIV and XV.

different forms of the same name of the same solar deity of the West; and that these different writings arose in different centers through the adoption of the cuneiform script of the Sumerians, whose scribes were the first to write upon clay for the Semites who entered the Tigro-Euphrates valley. The very absence of these names, generally speaking, is proof that the theory advanced is correct; although it is most surprising that sporadic occurrences of Babylonian names compounded with these elements in the names of the West, like *Ellil-bâni* in the Cappadocian tablets, should not be found. From this point of view, therefore, it must be acknowledged that the dependence of Canaan upon Babylonia in the period of the Exodus is grossly exaggerated. If the same claim had been made for the Hittites, more evidence would be found in the Amarna letters to substantiate it. Let me repeat, the *argumentum e silentio* is precarious, but when in the nomenclature of Babylonia the Hittite, the Mitannæan, and other West Semitic influences are so apparent, we have every right to expect to find traces of Babylonian influence, if what scholars have claimed is more than a conjecture. A fresh discovery may produce some of the required data, but still the position taken by the Pan-Babylonists cannot be maintained, for the evidence against it from many points of view is overwhelming.

It has been asserted that the Babylonian rule having been extended over this land by military conquest, not only the general culture and the alien language was enforced upon the people, but also the Babylonian system of law. Hammurabi having been suzerain over Amurru, it was quite natural to suppose that this great lawgiver established his laws there as well as in Babylonia, but this does not seem to have been the case. We find interesting parallels of customs practised among the patriarchs, as, for instance, the adoption of his servant, Eliezer, by Abraham; Sarah's giving Hagar to her husband for wife, and the subsequent treatment of her; Rachel giving her handmaid Bilhah to Jacob for wife, etc.

While there are no parallels for these practises in the Mosaic law, the existence of such Babylonian customs in the case of Abraham and his immediate clan is exactly what we should have expected; for he and his family had lived in Babylonia. It is, therefore, not necessary on account of these facts to assume that Hammurabi established his laws in Palestine. In truth, these very facts are merely interesting and important exceptions, assuring us that we have a veritable historical personage in the patriarch to deal with, and not the creation of a Hebrew fiction writer. His early life was spent in Babylonia, where he received his education. His emigration to Palestine and residence there as a shaykh among his people—a law unto himself—would not require us to suppose that he had forgotten his early training, and especially with reference to affairs of everyday life. At the same time, it would be unreasonable to suppose that the laws of Canaan were influenced by this petty shaykh, who we are told could gather only three hundred and eighteen men, which

INTRODUCTORY REMARKS 41

included those of several allies, when he went to recover Lot. Naturally, his own tribe, perhaps for generations, was more or less influenced by this Babylonian heritage; but contact for four or five centuries with the laws of Palestine, Egypt, and other lands gradually effaced the traces of this influence, as is evident by a comparison of Babylonian laws with the Mosaic code.

There are laws in both codes which are parallel. The *lex talionis* is common to both; but this continues to exist in Oriental lands at the present time, and doubtless will be found in other ancient Semitic codes that may be discovered. Without taking into consideration the laws arising from this barbarous law of retaliation, those which are similar can all be explained as coincidences which have arisen from similar conditions. Even a common origin for both cannot be proved. Not a few scholars have come to the conclusion that the points of agreement are due to independent development from the same primitive customs.[1]

Not only is it claimed that the people of the West adopted the language, the culture, the religion, and the laws of Babylonia, but that the literature was also absorbed as its own. The early stories in Genesis of the Creation, Sabbath, antediluvian patriarchs, and the Deluge have furnished the principal material for the support of this theory. Under these several heads this question will be discussed.

---

[1] For a fuller discussion of the question as to whether the Mosaic code is dependent upon the Hammurabi, see the writer's *Light on the Old Testament from Babel*, p. 223 ff.

It is not my desire to attempt to minimize the influences from the Tigro-Euphrates valley upon the culture of the neighboring nations in general, including Israel. Unquestionably such a civilization as the Sumerian, which, as far as we know, was highly developed as early as the fifth millennium B.C., and also the Assyro-Babylonian, exerted an influence upon neighboring peoples. What that influence was upon the center of the Semites from which the Semitic Babylonians came, of course, is a different question. It is well to bear in mind that while the Sumerians, on the one hand, greatly influenced the Semitic culture which was brought into the country, the Semites, on the other, had a great influence upon the Sumerians—not so much in their art as in their culture in general, for the Semite seems to have had little art worth imitating. By taking this more into account it is not improbable that many of the difficulties brought to light by the Halévy school will find their solution, for it is evident that the Semitic hordes, as they are called, which came into Babylonia greatly influenced the culture of that land. But beyond such influences as are due to commercial relations, and perhaps the script, it does not appear that the culture of Amurru, according to all that we know from the excavations and the monuments, was modified by Babylonian forces. In short, a careful consideration of the data at our disposal confirms the contention that many extravagant statements have been made concerning the indebtedness of Israel and the Western Semites to Babylonia.

Farther North it is apparent that the contact between

the Hittite and the Babylonian culture was closer. Whether the peoples will ultimately be shown to have had intimate relations with one another remains to be determined. Mutual influences, however, are shown by a study of the art.[1] The Babylonian influence upon that region is also apparent in the so-called Cappadocian tablets, as well as in the inscriptions from Mitanni. The influences from Babylonia or Shumer which found their way into Europe, doubtless, were largely transmitted through the medium of these peoples in Asia Minor.[2] In fact we are justified in looking for influences, at least in orthography, among all the nations that adopted the Babylonian script for their own language. This would include a people like the Amorites, in so far as they adopted the cuneiform script for their own language.

---

[1] See Ward, *Cylinders and other Ancient Seals in the Library of J. Pierpont Morgan*, p. 93, who finds Babylonian influences on the seal cylinders classed definitely as Hittites. This region he claims also gave in return more than one deity to the Babylonian pantheon.

[2] An interesting illustration of this is the Babylonian origin of the Platonic number, 12,960,000, which has been demonstrated by Aures and Adam, and recently discussed by Hilprecht, in *Babylonian Expedition*, Vol. XX, pt. 1, and by Barton, "On the Babylonian Origin of Plato's Number," *Journal American Oriental Society*, Vol. 29, p. 210.

CREATION STORY

It is a widely current theory that the cosmology of the Hebrews, as reflected in Genesis 1-2 : 4a, as well as in the prophets and in the poetic productions of Israel, was borrowed from the Babylonians; or, as an eminent scholar has expressed himself, "in fact, no archæologist questions that the biblical cosmogony, however altered in form and stripped of its original polytheism, is in its main outlines derived from Babylonia."[1] Certain scholars, however, while assigning for literary reasons all the passages in the Old Testament dealing with the so-called "Yahweh-Tehom myth," in their extant form, to a period as late as the exile, hold that there was a long development of the Babylonian myth on Palestine soil. Or, as another writer puts it, the Hebrew was founded upon the Babylonian soon after the invasion of Canaan.[2] "Yes," says Sayce, "the elements, indeed, of the Hebrew cosmology are all Babylonian; even the creative word itself was a Babylonian conception, as the story of Marduk has shown us."[3] Gunkel, followed by others, assumes a dependence

---

[1] Driver, *Commentary on Genesis*, p. 30. Barton, in his article on "Tiamat," *Jour. Amer. Orien. Soc.*, Vol. XV, 1-27, was one of the first writers to make an extended comparison between the Creation story of the Babylonians and Genesis. See also Jastrow, *Jewish Quarterly Review*, 1901, p. 622.

[2] Rogers, *Religion of Babylonia and Assyria*, p. 139.

[3] *Religions of Egypt and Babylonia*, p. 395.

of the biblical story in Genesis, including several remnants in the Old Testament, upon the Babylonian; but the former was separated from the latter by a long space of time. These represent the views generally adopted by writers on the subject, namely, that it was out of this circle of influences that the beginning of Israel's conscious thinking about the work of creation arose.

The sole argument of value that has been advanced for the Babylonian origin is, that in purely Israelite environment it is impossible to see how it should have been supposed that the primeval ocean alone existed at the beginning, for the manner in which the world rises in the Hebraic story corresponds entirely to Babylonian climatic conditions, where in the winter water holds sway everywhere until the god of the spring sun appears, who parts the water and creates heaven and earth. This cosmology, it is held, must therefore have had its origin in the alluvial plains, such as those of Babylonia, and not in the land of Palestine, still less in Syria or the Arabian desert. It also involves a special deity of spring or of the morning sun, such as Marduk was, and Yahweh was not.

It must be admitted that the fundamental conceptions expressed in the Hebrew story are not Palestinian in color, and that in all probability they are based upon a common inheritance. There is a Sumerian cosmology, the fundamental idea of which is that water is the primeval element, "for all the earth was sea." "In those days was built Eridu," which is in the region where the

46 AMURRU HOME OF NORTHERN SEMITES

Hebrews are generally regarded to have placed Eden, "out of which a river went, and from thence it was parted and became into four heads." The biblical cosmology not only places Eden in an alluvial plain, but it recognizes water as the primeval element. These ideas were held also by the Egyptians, Phœnicians and others, and it is altogether reasonable to assume that the Amorites and Aramæans had something similar. In so far, it must be admitted that the biblical story embraces cosmological conceptions similar to those found among the Sumerians and other peoples; but, as Pinches pointed out,[1] when he published this Sumerian legend which belongs to an incantation tablet, nothing is said in the fragment of a conflict between Marduk and Tiamat, the chief theme of the Babylonian legend.

The Marduk-Tiamat myth, which belonged to the Library of Ashurbanipal, is a late and elaborated attempt to explain the origin of things. The chief purpose of the legend, as it has been handed down, is the glorification of the god Marduk, who, as is well known, absorbed the prerogatives and attributes of the other gods, after Hammurabi caused him to be placed at the head of the Babylonian pantheon. That is to say, it is quite apparent that the writer composed the work from existing legends.[2]

Professors Jastrow, Sayce,[3] and others recognize two different schools of thought represented in the

---

[1] *Journal of Royal Asiatic Society*, 1891, p. 393 ff.
[2] Cf. Jastrow, *Rel. of Bab. and Ass.*, p. 407 ff.
[3] *Religion of Egypt and Babylonia*, p. 376.

myth, as is shown by the attempt to harmonize two conflicting conceptions. In the chaos symbolized by Tiamat is seen the relic of a cosmology which emanated from Nippur. This, it is claimed, was adopted and combined with the cosmology of Eridu that made water the origin of all things. With the Sumerian legend, found by Rassam at Sippara, before us, which doubtless came from Eridu, it seems quite clear that the Tiamat cosmology is entirely independent of it. But, contrary to the asserted claims, it cannot be said to have emanated from Nippur. I can agree with Professor Jastrow, who, in assuming the composite character of the Babylonian Creation story,[1] sees a version underlying it which represents a conflict between Ea and Apsu. This version, which emanated from Eridu, must be viewed as the establishment of order in place of chaos. But I fail to appreciate the claim made by certain Assyriologists that there is a distinct version of the episode which originated at Nippur, in which Bel or Ellil and Tiamat are the contestants. The arguments adduced in support of the theory are by no means conclusive. The transfer to Marduk of the prerogatives of Ellil cannot be used to explain the origin of all that belongs to Marduk, for that deity had an existence with proper attributes before Hammurabi conquered the Elamites, and was able to make him supplant the old *bêl mâtâti*, "lord of lands." This transfer of titles is definitely set forth in the myth, where

---

[1] See Nöldeke, *Festschrift*, p. 971 ff.

the compiler, in his efforts to glorify Marduk, bestows upon him all the attributes which belonged to other deities, as well as Ellil. But the statement which is used to prove that Marduk supplanted Ellil in this conflict is not justified by any known facts, namely, that the description in the fourth tablet of the equipment of the god—that is, the four winds, lightning, the storm chariot, and the storm weapons—only fits Ellil of Nippur, and is totally incongruous in the case of Marduk, because one is a storm-god and the other a solar deity. The argument, I repeat, has little or no weight, for, as will be seen below, Marduk, the god of light, is also a storm-god.[1] Adad, another representation of a solar deity in the West, is also the god of the winds and storms. The Sumerian *Nin-Girsu* is similarly a solar and agricultural deity. This is perfectly natural, as the sun recalls to life the slumbering powers of nature; but fertility is not only dependent upon the sun, but also upon rain.

This conflict between Marduk and Tiamat, as Zimmern[2] has held, is manifestly one of light against darkness, *i.e.* the god of light with the god of darkness, while the Sumerian symbolizes the establishment of order out of chaos. Ellil was not a god of light, but a deity of an altogether different character. Marduk, on the other hand, is pre-eminently a solar deity; and therefore, until some indisputable facts are produced to show that Marduk is not the original deity of the legend,

---

[1] See Jensen, *K. B.*, VI, p. 563.
[2] *Encyclopædia Biblica*, col. 733.

CREATION STORY

no other view should be countenanced. Further, in Part II it will be shown that Marduk (or *Amar-utuk*) has been introduced into Babylonia from the West.

Not only is Marduk, the god of light, an importation from the West, but also Tiamat, the mythical monster who personified the sea, the god of darkness. Scholars have indeed assumed that the Hebrew Tehom, translated "deep abyss," was borrowed from the Babylonian Tiamat. The latter, in Babylonian, is written in a form slightly different from *ti'âmtu* or *tâmdu*, the word for "sea," perhaps for the purpose of differentiation. This name, as far as published inscriptions are concerned, is confined to the primeval deity in the Marduk-Tiamat legend. The root to which this word, as well as *tâmdu* meaning "sea," belongs does not seem to be in use in Babylonian, except in these two words.

On the other hand, there are several roots in Hebrew הום, המה and המם, which mean "to make a noise, to confuse, to discomfit, to disquiet," to one of which Tehom probably belongs; though it is also possible, as Delitzsch[1] maintains, that there is also a root תהם. At the same time there are a number of derivatives, used in conveying ideas connected with "the deep sea, the abyss, confusion, the primeval ocean, the depth"; in fact, there is a wealth of synonyms, belonging to the very fiber of the Hebrew language and thought. And yet scholars have held that Israel borrowed the conception from the Babylonians, who, as far as is known, simply used

---

[1] *Prolegomena*, p. 113.

the word *tâmdu*, "sea," and also *Tiâmtu* in this legend. The chaos seems to be a Phœnician idea also (see below).[1]

The absence of the use of the stem in Babylonian, as above stated, considered in connection with these facts, makes the hypothesis that the Hebrews borrowed this idea from the Babylonians exceedingly precarious; in fact, it is unreasonable to assume that the Hebrew *Tehôm* is a modification of a Babylonian pattern. The deity furthermore is surely not Sumerian, at least it has not been proved to be such. To say, therefore, that the origin of the Marduk-Tiamat myth is to be found in a Nippurian version, originally known as Ellil-Tiamat, is utterly without foundation. With our present knowledge, the only conclusion at which we can reasonably arrive is, that this is an importation from the West.

The art as represented in the seal cylinders offers a weighty argument for the comparatively late introduction of this myth into Assyria. A characteristic design of the Assyrian period of the first millennium B.C. is the conflict between the deity of order and disorder, which has incorporated certain elements from the earlier cylinders depicting the battle between Gilgamesh and wild beasts. The composite production,

---

[1] In Pognon, *Inscriptions Mandaites des coupes de Khouabir*, Nos. 27, 33, the word is also found in Mandaic, which is an Aramaic dialect. The passage is בעומקיא תומיא תתאייא. Pognon (p. 65) suggests here a scribal error and proposes תוחמא, i.e., "black," but Professor Montgomery, who called my attention to the passage, translates "in the depth, the lower abysses." That is תומא is the same as the Hebrew תהום.

however, is intended generally to portray the conflict between Marduk and Tiamat, though it is important to bear in mind that the battle between Marduk and Tiamat is never represented in the early Babylonian art.[1] It belongs, as far as we know, to the Assyrian period, which therefore justifies us in seeking for the origin of the myth elsewhere than in Babylonia.

Such a conflict, as has been shown, is reflected in the Old Testament, where Yahweh put down a power of darkness. This, in fact, is a distinctive mark of Hebrew theology reflected throughout the Old Testament. It passed over into the New Testament, and has become the heritage of the Christian Church in the doctrine of the fallen angels. Under the guidance of a primeval leader, certain angels did not persevere in wisdom and righteousness, but apostatized, in consequence of which the chief, together with his followers, was banished to the eternal desertion of God. Augustine, it is interesting to note, maintained that the fall of these angels took place during the age represented by the second verse of Genesis, although he does not seem to have taken into consideration the passages in Job, Isaiah and the Psalms which refer to the conflict before the creation of the heavens and the earth between Yahweh and this primeval power of darkness, under the names Rahab, Leviathan, Dragon or Tehom and the "helpers."[2]

---

[1] Ward, *Cylinders and Other Ancient Seals in the Library of J. Pierpont Morgan*, p. 17.

[2] See Gunkel, *Schöpfung und Chaos*; Clay, *Light on the Old Testament from Babel*, p. 69.

The Israelitish conception of Sin presupposes influence from this primeval power of darkness and its allies. In Babylonian demonology the *lillu, eṭimmu, utukku,* and other destructive demons played an important rôle, but the knowledge of such a conflict between light and darkness, or between the god of light and the god of darkness, as far as is known in the literature of Babylonia, is confined to this myth.

Similar ideas seem to prevail also in the creation story of the Phœnicians. Eusebius, who reproduces what "a certain Sanchoniathon has handed down to posterity, a very ancient author who they testify flourished before the Trojan war,"[1] says the Phœnicians believed "that the beginning of all things was a dark and condensed windy air, or a breeze of dark air, and a chaos turbid and black as Erebus." In the Phœnician also Báαυ, *i.e.*, "emptiness,"[2] figured as a wife of ανεμος κολπια, from whom sprang the primeval men. The πνευμα, which is the same as the Hebrew *rûaḥ* in the chaos, also figured prominently in the Phœnician.

Nor is it strange that such a conception as a monster in the figure of a dragon should prevail in Israelite environment, as some have claimed, when we take a slightly broader view of the situation, and realize that we cannot localize this motive to certain inland cities occupied by Israel. Huge monsters are familiar

---

[1] See Cory, *Ancient Fragments*, p. 1.
[2] Cf. בהו of Genesis 1 : 2.

even now on the coast of Amurru. It is only necessary to refer to the story of Jonah, with its classical counterpart in the myth of Perseus-Andromeda, localized at Joppa, to meet this objection. In fact, according to our present knowledge, we must conclude that this idea is distinctively Palestinian, instead of Babylonian.

What is true of *Tiâmtu* can be said of other elements in the story, *e.g.*, the deity *Apsu* is also West Semitic. As will be seen in Part II, besides other elements *Laḫmu* and *Laḫamu* are the same.

The composite character of the Babylonian Creation myth being well established, and likewise that the amalgamation of the diversified elements took place some time prior to the establishment of Ashurbanipal's library, it seems reasonably certain that the two cosmologies, which are clearly distinguishable, represent a Semitic myth coming from the West, in which Marduk, the god of light, is arrayed against Tiamat, the god of darkness, and a Sumerian myth, presumably from Eridu, resulting in the establishment of order by Ea, as against the chaos, which is personified by Apsu.

Scholars are mistaken in assuming that there has been a complete transplanting of the Babylonian myth to the soil of Yahwism, or that the author of the biblical story had before him not only the cosmological system of the Babylonians, but that particular form which has been incorporated into the Assyrian epic. On the contrary, in the light of these discussions, it seems reasonably certain that the Western Semites who emigrated to Babylonia[1] carried their tradition with them to that land, which in time was combined with the Sumerian, resulting in the production discovered in the library of Ashurbanipal.

---

[1] On the movements from the West to the East in the third millennium B.C., see Clay, *Jour. Amer. Or. Soc.*, XXVIII, p. 142 ff., and Ranke, *O. L. Z.*, March, 1907. This has been accepted by Meyer, *Geschichte des Altertums*², I, § 436.

THE SABBATH

FOR some years a number of Assyriologists who have written upon the Sabbath of the Hebrews have reached the conclusion that not only "the word Sabbath is Babylonian indeed,"[1] but also that the institution originated in the Tigro-Euphrates valley. This is well expressed in the statement, "the Sabbath rest was essentially of Babylonian origin."[2] Or, as is asserted by Gunkel: "The history of religion, however, indicates that the observance of such a holy day is a remnant of an earlier time in the history of religion when man believed in gods, who according to their kind belonged to certain days."[3] Following are the facts upon which these conclusions rest.

In Rawlinson, *Inscriptions of Western Asia*, Vol. II, 32*a-b*, 16, the equation *sha-pat-tum* = *ûm nu-uḫ lib-bi* is found. This has been translated, "day of rest of the heart," and was supposed to contain the germ of the Hebrew Sabbath. The word *shapattum*, which can also be read *shabattum*, occurs in several syllabaries,[4] and has been explained by Professor Jensen to mean "appeasement (of the gods), expiation, penitential

---

[1] Rogers, *Religion of Bab. and Ass.*, p. 226.
[2] Sayce, *Religion of Egypt and Babylonia*, p. 476.
[3] Gunkel, *Israel und Babylonien*, p. 21.
[4] Cf. *Zeit. für Ass.*, IV, 274 f.

prayer," from a root which means "to conciliate." Professor Zimmern conjectured that the root means "to desist."[1] But up to the present the only explanation of *shabattum* from Babylonian sources is that it is a synonym of *gamâru*[2] and means "to be complete, to be full." And this meaning becomes perfectly intelligible in the light of the list of Sumerian and Babylonian days of the month published by Pinches,[3] from which we learn that *shabattum* was the name of the fifteenth day of the month; and considered in connection with the synonym *gamâru*, "to be complete," it doubtless had reference, as has been suggested, to the full moon in the middle of the month.

The idea originally advanced that *ûm nûḫ libbi* is a "day of the appeasement (of the gods)" or "the day for appeasing the anger of the deity" seems to be correct. This is further illustrated by personal names such as *Linûḫ-libbi-Ellil*, "May the heart of Ellil be appeased,"[4] or *Linûḫ-libbi-ilâni*,[5] or *Nûḫ-libbi-ilâni*.[6] It is not improbable that on the day *shapattum*, when the moon

---

[1] *K. A. T.*³, p. 593.

[2] Raw., V, 28, 14e-f. Hehn ("Siebenzahl und Sabbat bei den Babyloniern und im Alten Testament," *Leipziger Semitische Studien*) holds that *shabâtu* originally meant "to be complete," like *gamâru;* and that "to rest" is a secondary meaning. Another important treatise recently published on the Sabbath is *Sabbat und Woche im Alten Testament,* by Meinhod, who takes a different view.

[3] *Old Testament in the Light of the Historical Records,* p. 527.

[4] Cf. Clay, *B. E.,* vol. VIII.

[5] *B. E.,* vol. X.

[6] *B. E.,* vol. VIII.

was full, appropriate exercises were observed in conciliating the gods. But until some evidence is forthcoming, we cannot justifiably assume with Delitzsch (*Babel und Bibel*) that there was a "cessation (of work), keeping holiday," or that it was a rest day from human labor. No other conclusion, therefore, can be reached than that the Babylonians did not observe a day in every seven, that was called the *Sabbath*. And, until further light on the subject is produced, this must be clearly understood to be the fact.

The nearest approach to any resemblance to the Hebrew Sabbath that is to be found in the cuneiform inscriptions is on the so-called calendar of festivals for the intercalary month, Second Elul, and Marchesvan,[1] in which the duties of the shepherd or king are prescribed for the seventh, fourteenth, twenty-first, twenty-eighth and nineteenth days. While the other days of the month were regarded as favorable, these were regarded both as favorable and unfavorable. It runs thus:

"The seventh day is a holy day of Marduk and Ṣarpânitum, a fortunate day, an evil day. The shepherd of the great nation shall not eat meat roasted by the fire, which is smoked(?), he shall not change his garment, he shall not dress in white, he shall not offer a sacrifice. The king shall not ride in his chariot, the priestess shall not pronounce a divine decision, in a secret place the augur shall not make (an oracle); a physician shall not touch a sick man; (the day) is unsuitable for doing

---

[1] Raw., IV, 32-33.

58 AMURRU HOME OF NORTHERN SEMITES

business. The king shall bring his offering at night before Marduk and Ishtar, he shall make an offering; his prayer shall be acceptable to god."

This UD-ḪUL-GAL, or "evil day," observed not every seven days, but according to the lunar month, was not a day of rest for the people. As seen, there were some superstitious requirements demanded of the king on that day, but not of the common people. The investigations of Johns[1] show that in the Assyrian period in the eighth and seventh centuries before Christ (720–606), the seventh, fourteenth, twenty-first, and twenty-eighth days do not show any marked abstention from business transactions. The nineteenth day, however, does. In examining the dated tablets of the First dynasty of Babylon, *i.e.*, the time of Abraham, he concluded that there is a noticeable abstention on these days, but especially on the nineteenth day. Of a total of 356 tablets, the number dated on the first day of the month was 39; on the seventh, only 5; on the fourteenth, 5; on the twenty-first and twenty-eighth, each 8. Considering the month to have thirty days, the average for each day of the month would be 11 and a fraction.

Johns does not state whether his investigations show that other days besides the first of the month were especially auspicious for business transactions as determined by the dated contracts. If there were, the figures do not prove anything. In the Cas-

---

[1] *Expository Times*, XVII, p. 567.

site period the Temple Archives show that the average amount of business was transacted on those days as well as on the nineteenth. As Johns observes, however, most of the Cassite documents referring to the affairs of the temple may necessitate their being considered from another point of view. In the time of the First dynasty of Babylon and in the Assyrian period, the nineteenth day stands out as one upon which Sabbatarian principles as regards the doing of business may have been at least partially observed. It seems it might have been a certain kind of a holy day.

Besides this hemerology for the intercalary month Elul and Marchesvan, no further light on the subject has been recovered. In the Hammurabi Code of laws, or in fact in the thousands of tablets that have been published, scholars have not been able to find anything, beyond what has been discussed, which even by inference would seem to show that the Babylonians observed such a rest every seven days.

This hemerology, or religious calendar, was found in the Library of Ashurbanipal, and, knowing the nature of that Library, it is not unreasonable to assume that his scribes, having collected every kind of literature, ancient and modern, found in some section of the country that such a lunar day was observed by officials. Knowing as we do that Israel and Judah were carried to Babylonia and Assyria and placed in captivity, a custom that was practised in all probability for millenniums; and that this gave rise to many communities of Western Semitic peoples in the Euphrates valley, it is not

60 AMURRU HOME OF NORTHERN SEMITES

unreasonable to assume that at least in some places, where this element predominated, the Sabbath was observed in much the same manner as it was in Canaan. Knowing also that most of the published contracts of the First dynasty (when, as was noticed by Johns, there was at least a falling off of business transactions on certain days) come largely from a West Semitic center, it is not impossible to see here the results of a West Semitic influence.

Further, it must be noted that the Library of Ashurbanipal belonged to the century following the fall of Samaria and the deportation of Israel, during which century also Tiglathpileser (745–727 B.C.) took Ijon, Abel-Beth-Maacah, Janoah, Kedesh, Hazor, Gilead and Galilee, and all the land of Naphtali, and carried them captive to Assyria (2 Kings 15 : 29). That is, in the century prior to the time the Library of Ashurbanipal was gathered, thousands of Palestinian captives were brought to Assyria. This fact makes it altogether reasonable to expect to find some traces of the Hebrew institution.

Then also it can properly be assumed that other Western Semites besides the Hebrews observed the Sabbath, as, for example, the Aramæans, whence the Hebrews sprung.[1] As there is every indication in the Old Testament that the institution existed prior to Israel, and knowing how for centuries prior to the time of Ashurbanipal the Aramæans and Amorites

---

[1] Nielsen, *Der altarabische Mondkult*, shows that in Arabia there were seven and ten-day periods observed.

were the prey of the Eastern kings, we have every reason to expect to find some reflections of the observance of the day even from other than Hebrew sources in that land.

This much seems to be certain: The Sabbath as a day of rest, observed every seven days, has not been found in the Babylonian literature. While the hemerology of the late Assyrian period has preserved a knowledge of a regulation involving the king and his officials on the seventh, fourteenth, twenty-first, twenty-eighth and nineteenth days of two months of the year, which days were regarded as "evil days" and were to be observed according to certain restrictions in order to appease the gods, it cannot even be justifiably assumed at the present time (except perhaps for the nineteenth day) that there was any cessation from business of any kind or that there was a rest day for the people.

The very root from which the word is derived, if in use in the Assyro-Babylonian language, is almost unknown, and cannot be shown with our present knowledge to have the meaning "to rest, cease or desist." It is only necessary, on the other hand, for one to glance at a dictionary of Hebrew words to be impressed with the widely extended usage of the root *shabath*, "to cease, desist, rest," to which the word "Sabbath" belongs. And knowing what this institution was to the Hebrew, as is indicated in all the Old Testament codes—that it was not a day depending upon the lunar month, but was observed every seventh day, although there was in addition the new-moon festival which was also a day of rest; and further appreciating how extensive was the legislation concerning it—that it meant not only abstention from daily pursuits, but was a day of consecration, one which the people sanctified by a proper observance; that it was not an austere day for the king, so that the anger of the gods would be appeased, but a day of rest for slave, stranger, and even beast; and that it was an institution without parallel in ancient as well as in modern times, yes, the day *par excellence* among the Hebrews—it seems evident, without any elaborate discussion of the question, that the Pan-Babylonists, and others who hold similar views, are mistaken when they find the origin of the institution in Babylonia.

ANTEDILUVIAN PATRIARCHS

FOR some years Assyriologists have declared that the names of the antediluvian patriarchs of Genesis were borrowed from Babylonia, as represented in the antediluvian mythological kings in the list handed down by Berosus. Zimmern,[1] Hommel,[2] Jeremias,[3] Sayce,[4] and others hold that the names of the Hebrew list, in part at least, are direct translations of the Babylonian names. Some even hold that they are the work of a learned priest of the period of the Babylonian exile. Following is a list of the Chaldean kings as quoted by Berosus, from Eusebius.[5] The forms of the Armenian translation are here presented in Latin.[6]

1. Ἄλωρος, Aloros.
2. Ἀλαπαρος, Alaporus, Alapaurus, Alaparus.
3. Ἀμιλλαρος, Ἀμηλων, Almelon.
4. Ἀμμενων, Ammenon.
5. Μεγαλαρος, Μεγαλανος, Amegalarus.
6. Δαωνος, Δαως, Da(v)onus.
7. Εὐεδωραχος, Εὐεδωρεσχος, Edoranchus, Edoreschus.
8. Ἀμεμψινος, Amemphsinus.

---

[1] K. A. T.³, 539 ff.
[2] Proc. Soc. Bib. Arch., 1893, 243 ff.
[3] Das Alte Testament, etc., p. 119.
[4] Expository Times, May, 1899, p. 353.
[5] Chron. liber prior, edited by Schoene, p. 7 ff.
[6] See Zimmern, K. A. T.³, p. 531.

64 AMURRU HOME OF NORTHERN SEMITES

9. Ὠτιαρτης, Ἀρδατης, Otiartes.
10. Εισουθρος, Σισουθρος, Σισιθρος, Xisuthrus.

The first name, Ἄλωρος, is considered to be the equivalent of the Babylonian *Aruru*.[1] In the light of the discussion which is found in Part II, it is without doubt the name of the chief deity of the Amorites, which is written El-Ur or El-Or (אלור) in the recently discovered inscription of Zakir, published by Pognon.

These scholars all regard the second name, Ἀλαπαρος, to be equivalent to *Adapa*. It is, however, not necessary to resort to such violence, and especially when it can be translated as a good West Semitic name. The full name is as above, or as the Latin version has it, namely, *Alaporus*. An additional element must be recognized besides *Alap*, namely, the name of the god *Ûru*.[2] This would give us *Alap-Ûru*, "Friend or Ox of *Ûru*," with which we can compare the Babylonian name *Rîm-Sin*, "Ox of Sin," etc.[3] *Eleph* (אלף), which is a place name in Benjamin (Joshua 18 : 28), may also be compared.

These scholars have said Enosh, "man," the third name in the Hebrew list, is a translation of Ἀμηλων or *amêlu*, because the latter also means "man." The fuller form of the third name, Ἀμιλλαρος, must

---

[1] See Jeremias, *Das alte Testament*, p. 119.
[2] Zimmern (K. A. T.³, p. 531) recognized that the endings of several of the names were similar: "Die Endung ρος könnte dabei derjenigen in Ἀλωρος, Ἀμιλλαρος, Μεγαλαρος nachgebildet sein."
[3] In Kings, *Chronicles*, II, p. 17, *Rîm(AMA)* is written. Cf. also *Agal-Marduk*, "Calf of Marduk," etc.

ANTEDILUVIAN PATRIARCHS 65

naturally be considered in preference to the abbreviated form. And here again attention is called to the second element which is *Ûru*. This gives us instead of *Amêlu*, which is only part of a name, *Amêl-Ûru*, a common proper name formation. In this connection we must remember that the first element may be also West Semitic, for compare the name *Amal* (עָמָל) of a man in the tribe of Asher, which is from the stem meaning "to labor." It is, therefore, safe to conclude that both elements of the name are in all probability West Semitic.

The fourth name, Ἀμμενων, which is regarded as the equivalent of the Babylonian word *ummânu*, "workmaster," it is declared was translated into Hebrew and became Cain = *Qênan*, "smith." It seems, inasmuch as no such personal name as *Ummânu* exists among the more than ten thousand known Babylonian names, that we must look for another explanation.

The fifth name, Μεγαλαρος, does not seem to have been explained by Zimmern and Jeremias, but Hommel suggests[1] that it is a corruption of *Amilalarus, i.e., Amîl-Aruru*, "man of *Aruru*." Again, it should be said there is no need to alter the name in order to explain it. This can also be West Semitic, *i.e., Megal-Ûru*, for compare Mikloth (מִקְלוֹת), the name of a man in the tribe of Benjamin (I Chron. 8 : 32) and of a general in David's army (I Chron. 27 : 4).

The seventh name, Εὐεδωραχος, has been identified

---

[1] *Proc. Soc. Bib. Arch.*, 1893, p. 243 ff.

with *En-me-dur-an-ki* (written in Sumerian), the name of a mythological king of Sippar, who received revelations from his deity and ruled three hundred and sixty-five years. The king has been identified with Enoch, also the seventh in the list of the Hebrew patriarchs, "who walked with God," and lived before his translation the same number of years, namely, three hundred and sixty-five. While no connection between the names is suggested, there is good reason for supposing that these facts point to a common origin.

The eighth name, 'Αμεμφινος (*Amemphsinus*), Hommel[1] and other scholars think is a corruption of Amilsinus, *i.e.*, *Amêl-Sin*, "man of the moon-god Sin," and compare it with the eighth Hebrew name, *Methu-Salah*, "man of Salah or of the javelin." This, Sayce[2] suggests, is a variation of *Mutu-sha-Irkhu*, "man of the moon-god," which is equivalent to the Hebrew *Methu-sha'el*. These explanations and comparisons do not appear to be convincing.

The ninth name, Ωτιαρτης, which Alexander Polyhistor writes 'Αρδατης, is made equivalent by these scholars to *Ubar-Tutu*, the father of the Babylonian hero of the deluge. No effort is made to compare this name with Lamech, which is the ninth in the Hebrew list. It should be noted that the form given by Polyhistor may perhaps be nearer the original, in which case the first element in the name probably is the god *Ûru*, which frequently appears as *Âru* (see Part II). The

---

[1] *Proc. Soc. Bib. Arch.*, 1893, p. 243 ff.
[2] *Expository Times*, 1899, p. 353.

second element may be represented in the name *Dati*, a scribe of the time of Sargon, as well as in the name *Dati-Ellil*, the well known father of Sargon of Akkad. Compare also *Ardata*, a place name along the coast of the Mediterranean in the Amarna letters.

The tenth is that of the hero of the deluge, which is regarded as an epithet of *UT-napishtim*, the Babylonian Noah. Although no relationship between the names is apparent, the fact that the tenth name ends both lists with the diluvian hero points to some connection between them. And this gives rise to the usual question asked in connection with discussions of this character, Is the Babylonian derived from the Hebrew, or the Hebrew from the Babylonian, or have they a common origin?

As stated above, the view which has been widely accepted, is that a learned priest secured these legends from the Babylonians while in exile; that he translated the names into Hebrew, and appropriated the list for the history of his race. The conclusions which these scholars reach seem to demand that the Jews allowed an extensive influence to be exerted upon them by this polytheistic people, who had robbed them not only of their independence and the actual possession of their territory, but also even deported them and held them in bondage. That is, their kings and priests and people were torn from their ancestral home; their women and children were forced to endure the awful hardships entailed upon them in being transferred, after having been subjected to atrocious indignities of every imaginable character, and then held as slaves in this alien land. Is the theory reasonable that the priests, learned in their ancient cult and in their ancestral history, should have adopted at this time as their own antecedents these mythological kings of Babylonia, who, Berosus tells us, ruled, on an average, four hundred and thirty-two thousand years?

The Jews were carried to Babylonia by Nebuchadrezzar, and many were deposited in the vicinity of Nippur.[1] In the time of Artaxerxes I. and Darius II. the country seems to have abounded with them. While many returned to their own land, a large population continued to reside there. The Babylonian Talmud was written in that land by the descendants of those that remained. Naturally, if the Jews who returned to Palestine had been so extensively influenced by the Babylonian religion and history, we should suppose that the Jews who remained in the land certainly, by reason of their attachment for it, would have been influenced even more in this direction. But this does not seem to have been the case.

The spoken language of Babylonia when the Jews lived in exile was the Aramaic.[2] When they returned to Palestine they found that Aramaic, which was the *lingua franca* at that time of Western Asia and Egypt, was generally spoken in the land. To accept the conclusion of these scholars we are required also to explain

---

[1] See Clay, *Light on the Old Testament*, p. 403 ff.
[2] See Winckler, *Geschichte Bab. und Ass.*, p. 179; Clay, *Bab. Exp.*, X, p. 10, and *Light on the Old Testament from Babel*, p. 397 f.

why these late Hebrew priests or scribes should have adopted the language of the earlier period for these myths and legends which they are supposed to have introduced in Jewry, and why they interspersed their writings with many archaic forms. Did these religious innovators by so doing desire to give their borrowed stories an ancient appearance, and thus deceive the people by their literary forgeries?

As mentioned above, the fact that Edoranchus and Enoch, respectively the sixth of each list, both conversed with their deities, and the former ruled three hundred and sixty-five years, the same number that the latter lived on earth, and the further fact that the tenth and last of each list are the heroes of the deluge, seem to be points that cannot be considered simply as coincidences. But, as is further shown above, the argument that the Hebrew is a translation of the Babylonian is utterly without proof.

In the light of all these facts, the most reasonable conclusion seems to be, that inasmuch as most of the names can be explained as being West Semitic, they are such and not Babylonian. This follows from the fact that the chief deity of the Amorites (discussed in Part II), here written Ωρος, *Oros* and *Aurus*, figures in five of the ten names. Since the list of these mythological kings is headed by Ἀλωρος, "God *Ûru*," we must conclude that it was brought into Babylonia by the Semites from the West. It is perfectly natural that the Semitic Babylonians, who were not indigenous to Babylonia, but, as I maintain, in all probability were from *Amurru*, should have preserved after they entered Babylonia their ancient list of kings, headed by the name of their chief deity. This enabled them, naturally, to regard their rulers as having divine origin. Instead, therefore, of finding the origin of this legendary list of kings in Babylonia, together with their culture, it is to be traced back to a common stock of Semitic traditions, which had their origin in the great land *Amurru*.

DELUGE STORY

THE most important proof of the absolutely unquestionable dependence of the biblical narrative upon a Babylonian archetype that scholars have found is the story of the Deluge. Gunkel is right in saying that almost all Assyriologists and Old Testament scholars regard the Deluge story indubitably of Babylonian origin.[1] Delitzsch and others incline even to the opinion that the biblical author had the Babylonian legend before him, and that he translated and revised it. Even Rogers says that it is "quite clear that the material of the Hebrew narrative goes back undoubtedly to the Babylonian original."[2]

The Babylonian story of the Deluge is so well known that it is not necessary to recapitulate it here. The striking resemblances to the biblical story have so frequently been noted that they need not be repeated; nor is it necessary to emphasize the fact that they show a common origin for both narratives.[3] In so far all scholars are agreed.

Gunkel, however, taking the position generally held, thinks that those who are unwilling to agree that

---

[1] *Israel und Babylonien*, p. 16. Cf. also Jastrow, *Rel. of Bab. and Ass.*, p. 506.
[2] *Religion of Bab. and Ass.*, p. 209.
[3] See Clay, *Light on the Old Testament from Babel*, p. 84 ff., or other works of the same character.

72 AMURRU HOME OF NORTHERN SEMITES

the Hebrew account is dependent on the Babylonian, but who say that both are versions of the same event, have over-anxious temperaments. He claims that inasmuch as the stories coincide in so many minor details, they are related as narratives. To prove that the Israelitish story was borrowed from Babylonia, he sums up his views in his *Israel und Babylonien* (p. 19) in two arguments.

First, the great age of Babylonian civilization and of the deluge narrative as well; second, the frequent occurrence of floods is very natural in the flat plain of Babylonia, which lies close to the sea and is watered by two great streams.

The argument advanced by Zimmern, who holds also that the narrative was transplanted from Babylonia, its birthplace, is practically the same as the arguments of Gunkel. He says that the story, which was primitive, was indigenous in Babylonia, and was transplanted to Palestine; because the very essence of the Babylonian narrative presupposes a country liable to inundations, like Babylonia. He regards the story simply as a "nature myth," representing the phenomena of winter, which in Babylonia is a time of rain.[1]

These writers hold the theory advanced by Dillman, as well as by others, that there was a common Semitic tradition which developed in Israel in one way and in Babylonia in another, is to be rejected. Those who

---

[1] *Encyclopædia Biblica*, I, p. 1059. See also Driver, *Commentary on Genesis*, p. 107.

fail to be convinced that there was no such common source are accused by Gunkel of being possessed with anxious piety in a sad combination with a pitiful lack of culture.

Besides the eleventh tablet of the Gilgamesh epic, which contains the deluge story, three other fragments have been found. The one, which is too small to be of any value, belonging to the early age, refers to the Babylonian hero. The second, now in the library of Mr. J. Pierpont Morgan, was written in the reign of Ammizaduga, about 2000 B.C., and represents a god calling upon Adad to cause a destructive rainstorm, and Ea interposing in order to save the diluvian hero. There are indications that even this is a copy of an earlier tablet. Scheil, who has given an account of the tablet, thinks this story was current in Sippara. We, therefore, have a Babylonian version of a deluge, distinct from the other, several centuries prior to the time of Moses. A third is in the Berlin Museum. Moreover, early seal-cylinders clearly indicate that scenes from the Gilgamesh epic were favorite themes for the lapidary of Babylonia or Shumer in a very early period. It is not improbable that some represent a Sumerian Noah in his ark. But this only proves the antiquity of some of the elements of which the epic is composed.

It is a well recognized fact that the Gilgamesh series is a collection of stories which became the national epic of the late Babylonians. Its composite character has already been pointed out; the work of the redactor in combining the different elements being an accepted fact.¹ In the epic are found relics of ancient Sumerian mythology combined with Semitic sun-myths; and some of the latter at least, the writer claims, have come from an ancient stock of legends possessed by the Western Semites.

It is not a question whether Israel borrowed the Deluge story from this Babylonian composition, or the Babylonians from Israel, but whether the Semitic elements in the Gilgamesh epic are indigenous to Southern Babylonia (*i.e.*, to the Sumerians); or whether they had their origin with the Semitic Babylonians who entered the land; or whether they go back to that Semitic center from which they came. It seems that most of the theories on the subject which result in saying the Hebrews borrowed their story from the Babylonians emanate from a very contracted view of the situation; as if the only civilized peoples in Western Asia that possessed a literature or mythology were the Babylonians or Sumerians and Israel. That the Babylonian legend is of a great antiquity offers no difficulty. The almost universal character of a tradition of the event, which marked an epoch for ancient peoples, the writer thinks, is based upon the recollection of an actual inundation of an extraordinary character. The Babylonian and the Hebrew narratives, both of which can be said to belong to a comparatively late period in the history of man, have many points, as we have seen, in common. Doubtless the Sumerians also possessed a narrative,

---

¹ See Jastrow, *Rel. Bab. and Ass.*, p. 470.

which may yet be found, some of the elements of which are included in the Gilgamesh series; but which may have been a story altogether different in character from the Hebrew and the Babylonian.

A fact to be constantly kept before us is that the biblical account makes the ark rest upon the mountains of Ararat (*i.e.*, Urarṭu of the inscriptions), while the Babylonian fixes the place at Mt. Nisir. If Nisir is a mountain, east of the Tigris, across the Little Zab, as has been declared, it can be said to be in *Urarṭu*, for that country included the highlands north of Assyria. It is a question whether in ancient times *Urarṭu* included the lofty mountainous plateau now known as Armenia. But the point to be emphasized is that both the Hebrew and the Babylonian stories localized the second beginning of man's history, not only in the same region, but also outside of Babylonia.

The biblical story contains some features which are acknowledged to be distinctively Palestinian. These, it is claimed, made their appearance after the story reached Palestine and was appropriated by the Hebrews. They are "Noah," "the olive leaf," which is characteristic of Palestine; "the ark," instead of a ship, because there are no large navigable rivers in that land; and the beginning of the deluge on the seventeenth day of the second month, as that is the month the rains begin in Canaan, whereas the Babylonian deluge began in the eleventh month, the time the rains begin to fall in Babylonia. This latter is based on the fact that the epic was written on twelve tablets, which Rawlinson suggested represented the months; the eleventh tablet, therefore, corresponding to the eleventh month. There seems to be about as much proof for this assertion as if it were said that all books containing 365 pages represent the days of the year. Further, I fail to see that "Noah" is distinctively Palestinian. There is but one Noah known in the literature of Palestine, whereas the element Nûḫ is frequently found in Babylonian nomenclature. It would seem that the Pan-Babylonists have here overlooked an important argument.

The statement that "olives" are characteristic of Palestine is most interesting, but it would have been more correct to have said Palestine and Syria, or still more appropriately *Amurru*, for at Beirut and Tripolis there are olive groves five miles square. Little or nothing is known of the origin of the word "ark" (*tebah*), although some declare it is of Egyptian origin. These supposed features, due to Palestinian influences after the story was borrowed from the Babylonian, do not offer very weighty arguments in support of the theory that the Deluge story originated in Southern Babylonia.

The Babylonian epic, as stated above, is composed of Semitic and Sumerian elements, the latter, it seems, growing up especially at Erech. The stories are made to revolve about the hero, named Gilgamesh, who is either a sun-god or his representative. As Sayce has said, "The story of the Deluge, which constitutes the eleventh book, has been foisted into it by an almost violent artifice."[1] The scenes are shifted from Erech,

---

[1] *Rel. of Egypt and Bab.*, p. 423.

and the hero starts on a journey to his ancestor *UT-napishtim*, in order to learn the mystery of his apotheosis, and to be relieved of a loathsome disease.

A very prominent feature in the path of this celestial voyager, before he embarked upon the sea of death or darkness, which was the Mediterranean, was the gate of the setting sun. This was at the mountain *Mâshu*. Its entrance was guarded by monsters daily from sunrise to sunset. This would imply from the rising of the sun until it passed through the gate at even, when it was closed. Jensen properly considers that this mountain was in Amurru, near the shore of the Mediterranean,[1] and that perhaps it is to be identified with the gap made by the Lebanon and Anti-Lebanon mountains.

This gate is the place of the *êrib shamshi*, "the entering of the sun," or, to give its earlier Sumerian form, the place of *MAR-TU*, *i.e.*, "the entering in of *Mar*" (see Part II). In the Gilgamesh epic, of which the Deluge story is a part, the hero, who is a solar god, or the representative of that deity, is thus made to figure prominently in connection with the Western mountain of the world, in *Amurru*, "whose back extends to the dam of heaven, and whose breast reaches down to *Arallu* (Hades)." This association with the Western gate of the sun, located in the land of *Amurru*, points to indis-

---

[1] Cf. *K. B.*, p. 575 f. Jensen, *ibid.*, p. 467, as well as Hommel, *Anc. Heb. Trad.*, p. 35, had previously considered the mountain to be in Arabia.

78 AMURRU HOME OF NORTHERN SEMITES

putable connections with the great *Shamash* or *Ûru* of the Western Semites.

The name Gilgamesh seems to be Semitic, although most of the scenes of the legend are depicted at Erech (see page 142), in Babylonia. The syllabary published by Pinches[1] determined the reading of the name Gilgamesh for the late period, *i.e.*, *GISH-ṬU-MASH* = *Gi-il-ga-mesh*. This enabled scholars to identify the deity with the mythical king Γιλγαμος mentioned by Aelian.[2]

A fuller and earlier form of the name, however, has been found on a little square tablet in the University of Pennsylvania Museum,[3] referring to a building in Erech (which city figured so prominently in the legend), dedicated to a deity whose name is written ^dGISH-*BIL-GA-MISH*.

The final element of the name, it will be noticed, is written in three different ways, *MISH*, *MASH* and *MESH*. This looks as if the name is not Sumerian, but quite probably represents a Semitic element. In this connection we recall that the Nineveh temple *E-MASH-MASH* is written *E-MISH-MISH* in the Hammurabi Code (IV, 61). The element *MISH* is also in the name of the Nergal temple at Cutha, *E-MISH-LAM*; and *MASH* is in the name of the temple *E-UL-*

---

[1] *Bab. and Orien. Rec.*, IV, 1890, p. 264.
[2] See Sayce, *Academy*, 1890, 8, Nov., p. 24.
[3] The text was published by Hilprecht, *B. E.*, I, part 1, No. 26, and was first translated by Hommel, *P. S. B. A.*, XVI: 13. Poebel also found the name in texts which he recently published, cf. *B. E.*, VI, 2, No. 26, III: 6.

DELUGE STORY 79

MASH at Agade, etc. As Gilga-mesh is a solar deity and figures in connection with the mountain *Mâshu* (see also discussion, page 126 f, on *Sha-Mash, Di-Mash-qi*, etc.), a plausible conjecture is that the name of the deity of the mountain is contained in the name.[1] If this is true, the same element in temple names would show extraordinary influence from the West.

The name of the diluvian hero, the ancestor of Gilgamesh, whom he visited, and who related his experiences, has been a subject of considerable controversy for years. If not altogether it is partly Semitic; and there are good reasons for regarding it as containing an element foreign to the Semitic Babylonian, which probably is from the West. Many different readings

---

[1] The first element of the name is written *GISH-BIL-GA* and *GISH-ṬU* (or *TUN*). *GISH-ṬU* = *pâshu*, which Jensen translates "axe"; cf. *K. B.*, VI, p. 187; also Zimmern, *Ritualtafeln*, 141, note ζ. The ideogram *ṬU* also = *pa-la-qu* (cf. *P. S. B. A.*, December, 1880, Pl. 1f., li. 34). *Palâqu*, perhaps the same as *balâqu*, means "to destroy, kill, ravage" (cf. Muss-Arnolt, *Dic.*, p. 810), from which *pilaqqu*, "axe," is derived. In the Hammurabi period the name *Belaqu* occurs a number of times (cf. Ranke, *P. N.*); and in the Cassite period *Bilaqqu* (cf. Clay, *B. E.*, XV). With these names we can compare the biblical Balak (בלק). As a mere conjecture I would like to propose that the name *Gilgamesh* in view of the writing *gish Bilga-Mish*, means the "Axe of Mash." This when written in Sumerian appeared with the determinative which was pronounced, and in time became Semitized into *Gisbilga* and later became *Gilga*. The axe in the myth appearing frequently as his weapon (cf. also the representations of Adad-Teshup given by Jeremias, in Roscher), it is not an unreasonable conjecture. This being true, it is altogether reasonable to assume, especially in the light of other facts here considered, that Gilgamesh was originally Amoritish.

and explanations have been offered for the name.[1] The second element is clearly *napishtim*, but the first has been read *UT, Pir, Per, Ṣît, Shamash, Nûḫ*, etc. The sign *UD* has properly also the value *Bir*,[2] and the name can be read *Bir-napishtim*; and if so, perhaps it is an abbreviation for a name like *Bir-napishtim-uṣur*, "O Bir, protect the life"; like *Nabû-napishtim-uṣur*, a common formation among Babylonian names. This reading seems to be supported by the tablet now in the J. Pierpont Morgan Collection, which was discovered by Scheil, who found *Pi-i*[*r*] where he thought the name was broken away. This reading of the name would explain why the determinative for deity is omitted,

---

[1] *Pir-napishtim*, "offspring of life" (Delitzsch, Schrader, Jastrow); *Par-napishtim* (Haupt, Muss-Arnolt); *Ṣît-napishtim*, "the saved one" (Jensen, Jeremias); *Nûḫ-napishtim*, "rest of the soul" (Hommel, Ball); *Shamash-napishtim*, "sun of life" (Hommel); *Ûm-napishtim*, "day of life"; *UT-napishtim* (Jensen). Zimmern, *K. A. T.*[3], p. 545, thinks Jensen in translating "he saw (*ûta, ût*) the life," *i.e.*, "he found life," has finally solved the difficulty; but a parallel name in Babylonian nomenclature does not exist. The same is true of the other explanations. If *UT* or *Shamash* were considered to be deities, and the name regarded as a hypochoristicon for a name like *Bir-napishtim-uṣur*, as above, the difficulties are removed. Naturally some of the explanations are given on the supposition that the name is symbolical of the part played by the hero; but even in that case we should expect a regular formation.

[2] In Strassmaier, *Dar.* 365 : 20, the name of an individual is written *ᵈMUR-ibni*, and in *Dar.* 366 : 18, the same name is written *ᵈUT-ibni*, which must be read *Mur* or *Bir*. Inasmuch as *Mur, Mir, Bir*, etc., are variations of the same name (see below and *K. A. T.*[3] 443 ff.) the reading is plausible.

because *Bir* was regarded as a foreign god in Assyria; and in such instances, because of religious prejudices, the scribes frequently omitted the determinative (see Part II).

It should be added, however, that there is one difficulty in connection with this explanation. The fragment of the version in Berlin[1] gives the hero's name twice *U-ta-na-ish-tim*, which would support the reading *UTA* or *UT*, and the translation, "he saw or found life," perhaps symbolical of the part played by the hero. The element *na-ish-tim* then stands for *napishtim;* but, as far as is known to the writer, unless it be assumed that the scribe made the same mistake twice, this phonetic change is peculiar to the name, and is difficult to explain. Whether the scribe who copied the myth from an earlier tablet was familiar with the proper reading of the name remains to be seen. If he was not, it would be possible to explain his writing *U-TA* for *UT* otherwise. Besides the peculiar transmission of the name Gilgamesh, mentioned above, and the name *Enkidu* (usually read *Ea-bâni*), which is written *EN-KI-DU* and *EN-GI-DU*,[2] perhaps the writing *Uta-napishtim* also indicates a partial semitizing of a Sumerian writing.

This hero of the flood, as Prof. Zimmern has said,[3] must also have been a sun-god. *Bir* or *Shamash*

---

[1] See Meissner, *Mitteilungen der Vorderasiatischen Gesellschaft,* 1902, No. 1.

[2] This reading was communicated to me by both Ungnad and Poebel, who seem to have reached the same conclusion independently.

[3] *Encyclopædia Biblica*, I, Col. 1058.

would therefore be quite appropriate for the name. Moreover, in consideration of what follows in Part II, the name appears to show connections with the culture that came from the West. *Buzur-KUR-GAL*, the pilot of the ship in the Babylonian deluge story, now to be read *Buzur-Ûru*, also shows West Semitic influence, as the name is compounded with the chief deity of Amurru. Also, the gods which figured in the narrative are mostly those which are recognized as being different representations of the sun-god, brought into Babylonia from the West, prominent among them being *Shamash* and *Urra-gal*.

In view of these considerations, we may conclude that predominant elements in this and other parts of the Gilgamesh epic are connected with the sun-deity and the land of the Western Semites, and that the origin of the Semitic portion of the epic, which doubtless includes those features which are common to the biblical narrative, goes back to a West Semitic narrative, which is parent also to the biblical version.

We are, therefore, led to conclude, in the light of these facts, that the influence of Babylonia upon Israel or even Amurru has been greatly overestimated. In fact, exactly the reverse seems to be the case, *i.e.*, many of the elements of the Semitic Babylonian religion and literature are not indigenous to the land, but in all probability came from the West; at least they had their natural development in that part of Western Asia. The ultimate origin may belong elsewhere, but that does not affect these conclusions.

ORIGINAL HOME OF SEMITIC CULTURE

SOME scholars have held that Southern Babylonia was the original seat of the Semites, or of the Semitic culture; others say the eastern confines of Africa; still others Armenia; but the great majority of scholars hold that the interior of the Arabian peninsula or Southern Arabia was the cradle of the Semites.[1]

The one important argument in support of the Arabian theory, which has met with such wide acceptance, is that the Arabic represents the purest Semitic language. This seems to have little force, however, when we take into consideration that, as far as we know, there was no important center of culture in Arabia which would have experienced as rapid a development from what was primitive as would be found elsewhere under other conditions. It is the opinion of some scholars that the Ethiopic language is even purer than the Arabic; why not assume that Abyssinia is the cradle of the Semites?

The arguments advanced from a study of the social and economic conditions seem to be rather precarious. The earliest influence upon Babylonia from Arabia claimed by some scholars, is the time known as the First

---

[1] For a full discussion of the various theories on this question see Barton, *Semitic Origins*, pp. 1 ff.

dynasty of Babylon, about 2000 B.C. Even though it be admitted that the rulers of the First dynasty are Arabian, they came into possession of Babylonia many centuries after the Semites had entered that land; and, like the Cassite kings and their subjects, they did not, as far as has been shown, seem to have influenced the Babylonian culture. We therefore have no light from early inscriptions upon this mooted question, for the earliest from Arabia are the Minæan, which belong to about the fifteenth century B.C.

The Semites must have migrated to Babylonia at the latest in the fourth or perhaps fifth millennium B.C., entering from the North, and slowly but effectually crowding out the Sumerians. As the Semitic Babylonian is more closely related to the Aramaic and Hebraic (or Amoraic) than to the Arabic and Abyssinian,[1] it ought to follow that the Babylonian, Hebraic and Aramaic tongues were at one time the same language.

---

[1] Hommel, Ungnad, Brockelmann and others divide the Semitic languages into East and West Semitic. They maintain that the former, *i.e.*, the East Semitic, is represented by the Assyro-Babylonian. The latter, *i.e.*, West Semitic, is divided into South Semitic (Arabic and Ethiopic) and North Semitic (Hebraic and Aramaic). The separation of the Babylonian from the others into a separate class has been prompted largely by grammatical differences. These, it seems to me, must be explained as being greatly due to the influence of the Sumerian script and language. Linguistically the Babylonian is closer to the Hebraic and Aramaic than the other Semitic languages. The following classification seems preferable, namely: The North Semitic, which is represented by the Amoraic, Aramaic and Assyro-Babylonian, and the South Semitic, which is represented by the Arabic and Ethiopic.

ORIGINAL HOME OF SEMITIC CULTURE 85

If we account for the development of the Amorite culture before the fourth or fifth millennium B.C., we are so far removed from the time the Semitic cradle rocked that until we get some glimpses into the early history of this culture before this time, or even of the Arabic before what we now know, such purely hypothetical speculations can only be taken for what they are worth. There is, however, no support for the view advanced by some scholars, that the language of Palestine (known to us as Hebraic), in the days of Abraham, was simply a dialect of Arabia; or that in Abraham's time the Aramæans were still a part of the Arab race. Such theories are wholly baseless and absurd in the light of fact and tradition. If in the main my contentions are correct, a readjustment of the extravagant statements advanced is in order; and especially in view of what follows in Part II.

The inscriptions and archæological finds of cotemporaneous peoples have corroborated in a remarkable manner the early history in the Old Testament of the nations of antiquity, while at the same time they have restored the historical background and an atmosphere for the patriarchal period, so that even a scientist can feel that the old Book has preserved not only trustworthy traditions to be used in the reconstruction of the history of that period, but also the knowledge of veritable personages in the patriarchs. Nothing has been produced to show that they are not historical; and on the other hand every increase of knowledge, gained by the spade or by the skill of the decipherer, helps to dissolve the conclusions of those who have relegated the patriarchs to the region of myth.

An interesting discovery has recently been made by Prof. Arthur Ungnad, of the name "Abram" belonging to the age when the patriarch lived.[1] The fact that the name had not been found in the cuneiform literature, owing to the patriarch's sojourn in Chaldea, gave rise to many different views; for example, it was claimed that it was an idealized name created by a late Hebrew writer, and meant "The sublime father." The discovery of the name written in three ways, *A-ba-ra-ma*, *A-ba-am-ra-am*, and *A-ba-am-ra-ma*, puts this important question beyond any further discussion.[2]

The discovery of the divine name Yahweh in cuneiform literature also has important bearings on the point under discussion. Contrary to the views of those who hold the Kenite theory concerning the origin of the worship of Yahweh, or that it came from a Canaanitic *Jâhû*, or from the Babylonian *Ea*, or that it is a development from a tribal polytheism into henotheism and then into monotheism, etc., for which there is no historical proof, the Old Testament furnishes the only light on the subject, which is that the name and worship of Yahweh came from the Aramæans. And as Abraham and his descendants, as well as his ancestors, were Aramæans,[3] it follows that the name and worship of Yahweh was familiar to the Aramæans.

---

[1] See *Bei. zur Ass.*, VI, 5, p. 82.
[2] See also Part II.
[3] See Appendix on Ur of the Chaldeas.

ORIGINAL HOME OF SEMITIC CULTURE 87

The investigations of Dr. William Hayes Ward[1] in connection with ancient seals have led him to the conviction that among the figurative expressions under which Yahweh is represented in the Old Testament, there are those which point to an Aramæan origin. This conclusion is evidenced by the symbolic representations under which the Aramæan deity Adad appears in ancient art.

The worship of Yahweh in the Old Testament is largely identified with the mountains; so, for example, the Syrians, in explaining their defeat to Benhadad, said concerning Israel's deity, "Their god is a god of the hills" (I Kings 20 : 23). The stories of Sinai, Horeb, Moriah, Carmel and Paran further testify to this. Yahweh is represented also as a god of storms, thunder and lightning, as is shown by many passages in the Old Testament, particularly in the Psalms and Prophets. He is frequently regarded also as a god of battles: "Yahweh is a man of war," the god of hosts. And further, Yahweh was represented symbolically in the art as the calf or young bull.[2] The golden calf that Aaron made, as well as the shrines at Bethel and Dan, so vehemently denounced by Hosea and Amos, are indicative of this.

The same characteristics are found in the art depicting the Aramæan Adad, who in the language of the prophet concerning Yahweh, "treads on the high places of the earth." He is the god of the clouds, thunder, lightning, rain, storm, deluge, etc. In Babylonian art he

[1] "The Origin of the Worship of Yahwe," in the *Amer. Jour. of Sem. Lang.*, XXV, p. 175 ff.
[2] *American Journal of Semitic Languages*, p. 181.

is represented as carrying a thunderbolt. As the god of war, he carries the bow, club and ax. When Adad is represented in his complete form, he holds in his hand a cord attached to a ring in the nose of a bull or wild ox. He is appropriately designated "the divine heavenly bull (*DINGIR GUD AN-NA*), the god of Amurru."[1] These distinguishing marks have led Dr. Ward to remark that "he cannot help believing that he (Adad) was the pagan Yahweh before Yahweh emerged as the universal god of monotheism;[2] and again, "it is not unlikely that the monotheistic worship of Yahweh originated in that of Addu."[3]

Naturally there is no more proof for saying that the worship of Yahweh is derived from that of Adad, than that the worship of Adad came from that of Yahweh. Although we are better acquainted with the worship of Adad from extra biblical sources of the early period, because the deity was adopted into the Babylonian pantheon, still it would be safer perhaps to say that these characteristic marks which both deities have in common point to their Aramæan origin; and especially as the Old Testament associates Yahweh with the Aramæans, and also because the inscriptions clearly show the same source for the worship of Adad.[4]

---

[1] *Découvertes*, XXX, 10.

[2] See *American Journal of Semitic Languages*, XXV, p. 185.

[3] See *Cylinders and other Ancient Oriental Seals in the Library of J. Pierpont Morgan*, p. 19.

[4] *Amurru* is also the "Lord of the Mountains," *MU-LU ḪAR-SAG-GA GIT*, i.e., *be-lu sha-di-i* (see Part II). This is further proved by the use of the ideogram *KUR-GAL* for *Amurru*, which means "Great mountain."

ORIGINAL HOME OF SEMITIC CULTURE 89

For some years certain scholars have consistently maintained that the divine name was to be found in several personal names of the Hammurabi period, as *Ja'wi-ilu*, etc.[1] Few, however, accepted this conclusion. But if the name was used prior to the age of Abram, as is inferred from the Old Testament, we should expect to find it in the early cuneiform literature, as well as the names of other Aramæan deities. This has turned out to be the case.

The name of Yahweh is found on a tablet said to be from Kish, in the reign of Rim-Anum, who ruled in the latter part of the third millennium B.C. The tablet is in the Morgan Library Collection, and will be published by the Rev. Dr. C. H. W. Johns, Fellow of Cambridge University. It is found also in another unpublished tablet, dated in the reign of Sumu-abum of the Hammurabi dynasty, which is in the possession of Prof. Delitzsch, of the University of Berlin. In both the name occurs in the oath formula.

The two deities usually mentioned in the oaths of the contract tablets from Kish are *Zamama* and *Urash*. In these two tablets *Ja-wu-um* takes the place of *Urash*. *Urash*, the god of Dilbat, is in all probability a Western deity.[2] *Za-am-ma* (or *Za-mal-mal*), the god of Kish, which is another form of *NIN-IB*, is also a Western deity.

These tablets, like those from Dilbat and Sippar, contain names of Western Semites, which make it

---
See Appendix on the name Yahweh.
[2] See Part II.

quite reasonable to expect such a variation as the use of the name Yahweh, if, as represented, the deity was Aramæan or West Semitic.

But, as a matter of fact, the name Yahweh, when compounded with elements in proper names, is found in the early literature in connections which also point to Aramæan or Amoritish origin. It is claimed in the discussion of the name and native country of Sargon[1] that he was a Western Semite, perhaps an Aramæan. The name of his great-granddaughter is *Lipush-Jaum*. According to our present knowledge, the only conclusion at which we can arrive is that *Jaum* represents the name Yahweh.[2] Further, the name of the First dynasty, *Ḫali-Jaum*, son of *Jawum*,[3] also contains this element. *Jawum*, which at least is the exact form of the divine name, together with *Ḫali-Jaum* are foreign names, and in all probability West Semitic.

In considering these different facts in connection with the name and worship of Yahweh, it seems that the Kenite, the Babylonian, the Canaanite, and all other theories must give way to that which is gathered from the Old Testament, namely, that the worship of Yahweh came from the country of the ancestors of Abram, the Aramæan. Recent discoveries thus furnish a greater antiquity for things biblical than is usually accorded to them, and point to the ancestral home of Abram, *i.e.*,

---

[1] See Appendix on the name Sargon.
[2] See Appendix on the name Yahweh.
[3] See Ranke, *Personal Names*, p. 114.

Aram, which was identified closely with Amurru, instead of Babylonia, as the source of Israel's culture.

It is necessary, therefore, to differ radically from even those who, like Professor Rogers, say that "the first eleven chapters of Genesis in their present form, as also in the original documents into which modern critical research has traced their origin, bear eloquent witness to Babylonia as the old home of the Hebrew people, and of their collection of sacred stories."[1] But, let me add, in appreciation of what the same writer says, even when he includes those elements which he thinks were borrowed from the Babylonians: "When. all these are added up and placed together, they are small in number and insignificant in size when compared with all the length and breadth and height of Israel's literature"[2] But the writer ventures to go even farther and to claim that the influence of Babylonian culture upon the peoples of Canaan was almost *nil*.

The story of Babel in Genesis at this point becomes especially interesting; for in it we may see a reflection as handed down by the biblical writer of the movement of the Semites from the West, who made Babel a prominent center. "As they journeyed East they found a plain in the land of Shinar." Here these mountaineers used "brick instead of stone," to which they had been accustomed in their native land; and "bitumen" instead of "mortar." This became naturally a city

---

[1] Rogers, *Religion of Bab. and Ass.*, p. 219.
[2] Rogers, *ibid.*, p. 226.

sacred to their chief deity, *Amar*, whose name the Sumerian scribes wrote in the cuneiform script, *Amar-uduk*.

It has been asserted that the *ziggurrats* or towers in Babylonia were preceded by tombs of the gods in the center of fire necropoles. This may be correct, but the name *ziggurrat* points to a Semitic origin for the tower. Also the idea of the *ziggurrat* being the representation of a mountain surely originated with a people from a mountainous district.

PART II

AMURRU IN THE CUNEIFORM INSCRIPTIONS

RECENT investigations on the part of the writer have resulted in the conviction that most of the deities of the Semitic Babylonians, which have been recognized by scholars as original sun-gods, had their origin in the great solar deity of the Western Semites, known as *Amar* or *Mar* and *Ûr*, which was written in the script of the West, אמר or כר and אור, or ור, also known as שמש. This deity, after having been transplanted to Babylonia by the Semites, appeared under different written forms in different localities, as *NE-URU-GAL* at Cutha, *AMAR-UTUG* at Babylon, etc. This is due to the fact that the Semites adopted the non-Semitic cuneiform script of the Sumerians. These Sumerian forms in time were semitized and became *Nergal* and *Marduk*, as the Sumerian *EN-LIL*, "Lord of the LIL," became *Ellil* and the Sumerian *NIN-GAL*, "Great mistress," became *Nikkal*, etc. With later streams of immigration coming from the West, as, for instance, in the Nisin dynasty (third millennium B.C.), the name in its original form continued to be brought into the country; but coming in when the early Sumerian forms of the Semitic names, as well as the religion, had been babylonized, they were treated as distinct deities. These, however, were not admitted at once into the

Babylonian pantheon of gods, but were treated for centuries as alien deities, as is shown by the fact that the determinative for deity in many cases was omitted.

Naturally an important point to be determined is that these movements from the West actually took place. In a paper read before the American Oriental Society in Philadelphia (Easter week, 1907) the writer referred to the fact that at the time of the First dynasty of Babylon (2000 B.C.), the personal names show that the country was filled with foreigners, notably Western Semites; and also endeavored to show that the names of the kings of the Isin dynasty (third millennium B.C.) indicate West Semitic influence upon Babylonia, and that the capital of this dynasty doubtless was a stronghold of that people. Before the paper appeared in print, Dr. Hermann Ranke, of Berlin, appears to have reached similar conclusions from an entirely different point of view. He called attention to a date on a tablet which he believed referred to the invading Amorites at the time of Libit-Ishtar, a ruler of this same dynasty.[1] The preceding dynasty, namely, that of Ur (*Urumma*) was Sumerian. In the reign of Gimil-Sin we learn that the king built "the wall of the country of the West," which was called *Murik Tidnum*, "the wall that wards off the *Tidnu*." As we shall see below, *Tidnu* is another name for the land of *Amurru*. This fact points to active interference on the part of the Amorites already at this time. As is usually understood, the rulers of the pre-

---

[1] See *O. L. Z.*, March, 1907, also Meyer, *Geschichte des Altertums*, I, § 416.

ceding dynasties were Semites, and were not indigenous to the land but came from some Semitic quarter. This the writer holds was *Amurru*.

As is known, *Amurru*, the name of the land, occurs in the inscriptions as early as the time of Sargon, king of Akkad.[1] The title of the early Sumerian rulers, *LUGAL AN-UB-DA TAB-TAB-BA*, and its Semitic equivalent, *shar kibrat arba'im*, which being translated means "king of the four quarters," implies suzerainty over this land. Gudea mentions two mountains of *Amurru*, namely, *Subsalla* and *Tidanu*, *i.e.*, *Tidnu*, by which the entire land apparently became known. The kings of the Ur and Nisin dynasties also ruled over the land. *Kudur-Mabug* in an inscription used the title *ADDA KUR-MAR-TU*,[2] "suzerain of *Amurru*.[3] This title, therefore, included sovereignty over the region ruled by the five kings mentioned in the four-

---

[1] See especially *Amurram(MAR-TU-am)*, *V. B.*, p. 225, and Meyer, *Geschichte des Altertums*, § 400.

[2] Rawlinson, *Inscriptions of Western Asia*, I, p. 2, No. III.

[3] The fact that *Kudur-Mabug*, otherwise known as *ADDA Emutbal*, called himself *ADDA MARTU* in the votive inscription dedicated to *Nannar*, has caused certain scholars to conclude that *MAR-TU* is not the so-called "West-land" of the shores of the Mediterranean, but is the name of a Western district of Elam, and probably another designation of *Emutbal*. It surely does not follow because a ruler used a different title in another inscription that the one must be synonymous with the other. Compare the change in the titles of Sargon and Dungi referred to below; or the fact that Hammurabi in some inscriptions calls himself "king of Babylon," and in one found at Diarbekir, "king of *Amurru*." Before accepting the name *MAR-TU* for West Elam, where a non-Semitic language was spoken, other proof must be forthcoming.

98 AMURRU HOME OF NORTHERN SEMITES

teenth chapter of Genesis. Later it became the possession of Hammurabi after his thirty-first year. In an inscription found at Diarbekir, the single title used by Hammurabi is "king of *Amurru.*"[1] During the First dynasty of Babylon many Amorites seem to have dwelt in the vicinity of Sippar, where there was a city called *Amurrû*. But we cannot follow Toffteen,[2] and those who hold the view, that the Amorites of the West emigrated from this place through pressure from Elam, and in this way the name was transferred to the West-land. This was a settlement of Amorites, like the Jewish settlement in the vicinity of Nippur during the captivity and after it, having been deported perhaps to that locality by a predecessor of Chedorlaomer (see Appendix on "Ur of the Chaldees").

This title passed down to his successors; among them Ammi-ditana is mentioned as having enjoyed it. Nebuchadrezzar I, Tiglathpileser I, Ashurnaṣirpal and Shalmaneser II refer to the land. Adad-nirari III conquered Khatti (Hittite land), Amurru, Tyre, Sidon and Omri (Israel). Sargon includes the Khatti in the "widely extended" land of Amurru, as well as Phœnicia, Philistia, Moab, Ammon and Edom. Ashurbanipal, Nabonidus and Cyrus also refer to the land.[3]

In the first and second millenniums B.C., the cuneiform inscriptions lead us to believe that Amurru had become a general appellation for Syro-Palestine, a por-

---

[1] See Sayce, *Archæology of the Cuneiform Inscriptions*, p. 143.
[2] *Researches in Assyrian and Babylonian Geography*, p. 30.
[3] See Toffteen, *ibid.*, p. 29.

tion of which was controlled by the Hittites; that is, the borders of Khatti seem to have been extended so that the rule embraced a considerable portion of what was once Amurru. In the time of Rameses II the Hittites, we learn, occupied the land of *Amur*. If, as a people, the Amorites ever dominated politically that land in an organized manner, their history belongs to the third or earlier millenniums. It is not unlikely that the order was always that of petty principalities, and that the name was generally regarded as a geographical designation of the land.

To Delattre[1] belongs the credit for having determined the Semitic reading *Amurru* for the Sumerian *MAR-TU*, instead of *Aḫarru*. Jensen[2] further substantiated the reading. The passage in a hymn published by Reisner,[3] namely, $DINGIR^4$-MAR-TU(-E) = ^{d}A-mur-ru, as is known, fully and definitely corroborated the reading. It would seem that very early *DINGIR-MAR-TU* and *KUR-MAR-TU* were read respectively the deity and country of the Amorites, as the transliterations, especially for the latter, *i.e.*, *Amurrû*, occasionally contain an additional final vowel, as if an *adjectivum relationis*.

In the earliest inscriptions, as we have seen, *MAR-TU*

---

[1] *Proceedings of Society Biblical Archæology*, 1891, p. 233 ff.

[2] *Zeitschrift für Assyriologie*, Vol. XI, p. 304, 5.

[3] *Sumerisch-babylonische Hymnen*, 24, Rev. I1, 5, etc.

[4] For the benefit of those who have not paid attention to Semitics, it might be mentioned that what is printed in capital letters like *DINGIR*, in italics, is Sumerian, and what is in smaller type like *ilu*, is Semitic Babylonian.

is the Sumerian ideogram for the name *Amurru* and the question arises, Why was this combination of characters selected to represent this country?

MAR, which is also frequently used as the name of the land alongside of *MAR-TU*,[1] is doubtless, as has been suggested, a shortened form of *Amar*, which became *Amur* under the influence of the labial.[2] *MAR* is one of the names of the sun-deity, as will be shown in the pages which follow. As a deity in personal names under that form in the Assyrian period, it occurs in *Mar-larimme, Mari-larim, Mar-bi'di, Mar-irrish, Mar-ṣuri*, etc.,[3] and also in such names as כרברך, etc., from West Semitic inscriptions discussed farther on. *TU* in Sumerian has the value *erêbu*, "to enter."[4] *MAR-TU* like *UD-TU* (or *êrib shamshi*), therefore, means *êrib Mar*, "entering in of *Mar*" (or *Amar*, i.e., "the setting light or sun"). This, of course, shows that *Mar* (= *Amar*) meant the "sun" originally, and in all probability was the chief deity, the Shamash of the Amorites.[5] To the Babylonian it was also the name of the land, for *Amurru* was the "land of the setting

---

[1] Cf. Zimmern, *K. A. T.*³, p. 415, note 1; also Tofteen, *Ass. Bab. Geog.*, p. 32. *MAR* has also the value *Amurru*, "West," alongside of *IM-MAR-TU*, cf. Kugler, *Sternkunde und Sterndienst*, p. 23.

[2] Rawlinson, II, 35 : 19, is perhaps to be restored [*MAR*]-*TU-u* = *A-ma-rum*; but cf. also the following line *A-ru* = *A-ma-rum*.

[3] See Johns, *Assyrian Deeds and Documents*.

[4] Cf. Prince, *Sumerian Lexicon*, p. 233.

[5] In Job 31 : 26, אור, "sun," is used instead of *shemesh* in parallelism with the "moon."

sun." Here properly the Gilgamesh epic should be recalled which refers to the gate of the setting sun, as being located in the land of *Amurru* at the mountain *Mâshu*.

In the earliest known inscriptions of the Sumerians and Babylonians the West Semitic *Mar* (or *Amar*) figures prominently, as is determined by the fact that the Sumerians wrote *MAR-TU* for *Amurru*. This shows that the sun-cult of the West was well established in the earliest known period of Babylonian history, and doubtless already had had a long history of development.[1] This might have been inferred already from the fact that the earliest known rulers extended their conquests into the region *Amurru*.

Besides this ideogram for the deity *Amur* or *Amar*, another sign occurs in the Neo-Babylonian proper names, which usually has been read *ṢUR*, *Marduk*, etc. It occurs in *Amar-ra-pa-'*, *Amar-a-pa-'* (perhaps the same as the previous name), *Amar-na-ta-nu* (son of *Addu-taqummu*[2]) and *Amar-sha-al-ti* (whose son, *Ilu-arapa*,[3] also bears a West Semitic name). About one-half of the names with *Amar* are compounded with foreign or West Semitic elements, indicating unmistakably that the deity *Amar* belongs in the West.

In *The Babylonian Expedition of the University of Pennsylvania* (Vol. X, pp. 7 ff.), the writer showed that in the Aramaic reference notes scratched on the clay

---
[1] See also Part I.
[2] See Tallqvist, *Namenbuch*.
[3] See Clay, *B. E.*, Vol. VIII.

tablets, the transcription אור, which occurs in several names, represented *KUR-GAL*; and that these characters are to be read *Amurru* = *Awurru* (or *Ûru*), and not *Bêl* or *Shadû-rabû* as generally read. Such names as *Amurru-ḫaḫa*,[1] *Amurru-natannu*,[2] *Amurru-nazabi*,[3] *Amurru-shama*,[4] containing foreign elements in connection with the name of the deity *Amurru*, seem to substantiate the view that *Amurru* (or *Ûru* as in *Ûru-milki*[5] and *Milkûru*,[6] see below) was a foreign god.

Peiser[7] verified completely this identification, by showing that the name *MAR-TU-êrish*, *KUR-GAL-êrish*, and *Amurria* belonged to a single individual, the latter being a hypochoristicon with the ending *ia*, like "Sammy" from *Samu-el*. In other words, we get the formula *MAR-TU* = *KUR-GAL* = *Amurru* = אור (or *Ûru*).

Of special interest and importance is the fact that a single ideogram has the values *Akkadû*, *Amurrû* and *Urṭû*:[8]

Uri	BUR-BUR	Akkadû
Tidnu	BUR-BUR	Amurrû
Tilla	BUR-BUR	Urṭû

---

[1] Strassmaier, *Nbk.* 66 : 3.
[2] *Nbk.* 459 : 4.
[3] *Nbk.* 132 : 2.
[4] *Nbk.* 42 : 5.
[5] *K. B.*, II, p. 90.
[6] *Amarna Letters*, K. B., V, 61 : 54, etc.
[7] *Urkunden aus der Zeit der dritten babylonischen Dynastie*, p. VIII.
[8] See Delitzsch, *Ass. Les.*³, Syl. B, 72–74, and Weissbach, *Miscellen*, p. 29.

AMURRU IN CUNEIFORM INSCRIPTIONS 103

In another text, instead of *Tidnu* = *Amurru*, is found *Ari* = *Amurru*.[1] *Tidnu* is the name of a mountain in Amurru mentioned already in the time of Gudea (see above).[2] *Tilla*[3] is the name of a deity, as well as the name of a land in the region called *Urṭu* or Armenia.

In other words, the usual ideogram for the country *Ûri* or Akkad (*i.e.*, Babylonia) stood also for the countries *Âri* or Amurru and *Urṭu* or Armenia. Here should be mentioned again the monument of Hammurabi, found at Diarbekir, in Southern Armenia, in which the single title used is "King of *Ûru* (Amurru)."

---

[1] See Meissner, *Ideogramme*, No. 5328.

[2] Cf. *Vor. Bib.*, I, p. 70.

[3] *Tilla* is the name not only of the land but of a deity, cf. *Ḫu-di-ib-Til-la*, *Ash-tar-Til-la* and *Ta-i-Til-la* of my *B. E.*, vol. XV, and *A-qar-Til-la* of *B. E.*, vol. XIV; also cf. *Te-ḫi-ip-Til-la* and *Ishtar-kí-Til-la*, Pinches, *Journal of the Royal Asiatic Society*, 1897, p. 589 ff., and *Ti-mi-Til-la*, *Orien. Literaturzeitung*, 1902, p. 245. Cf. also *Me-Tilla*, chief of the Hittites in the treaty of Rameses II. Additional names compounded with *Tilla* have been published recently by Ungnad (*B. A.*, VI: 5, p. 14), *I-ri-ir-Til-la*, *Mish*(?)-*ki-Til-la*, *Shur-ki-Til-la* and *Shi-mi-Til-la*. Others will appear in my forthcoming volume of Temple Documents. Bork rightly regarded the first name mentioned above to be Mittannæan, cf. *O. L. Z.*, 1906, p. 591. This seems to be corroborated by the names which are quoted from the tablet published by Pinches. My attention has been called by Dr. A. T. Olmstead to a place *Tillah*, mentioned by Layard (*Nineveh and Babylon*, p. 41), at the junction of the East and West Tigris, which is on the direct route from Assyria to the Lake Van district. Another site *Tela* is mentioned by Ashurnasirpal (I, li. 113 f.), which later was called Constantia and now Viranshehir, between Urfa and Mardin and S. E. of Diarbekir. The ruins are important, but not early. Olmstead thinks the Assyrian site of this city is to be fixed to the N. W. at the near-by mound of Tell Gauran.

An important argument for the movement of the Amorites into Babylonia is to be found in this fact, that the name of that land in the third and fourth millenniums before Christ, after the Semites had entered, is the same as the name of the country from which they came, or, in other words, the Amorite land called *Amurru* or *Ûru* was geographically extended so that it included that part of the Euphrates valley occupied by the Semitic Babylonians.

The fact that Akkad or Northern Babylonia is called *Uri*, and that Amurru is called *Ari*, raises the question whether there is a connection between *Amurru* and *Uri* or *Ari*. We have seen that in the late period the Aramaic equivalent for *Amurru* which is scratched on cuneiform tablets is אור. The representation of the Babylonian *m* by the Aramaic *w*, or *vice versa*, is well known; for example, שוש is written in Aramaic for *Shamash*, סיון for *Simanu*, and ארגן for *argamanu*. Perhaps the most striking illustration of this is the transcription of the Hebrew יהוה by *Jâma* in Babylonian.[1]

Naturally it is possible that the Aramaic equivalent אור for Amurru was pronounced by the Aramæans *Awur*, although ordinarily *w* in such instances became a vowel letter, as *'ôr* for אור, "light," etc. In Babylonian the elision of a *w* between two vowels, after which a monopthongizing of the vowels takes place, is well

---

[1] See Appendix on the name Jahweh. The phonetic change of *m* to the semi-consonant *u*, after which it frequently disappears, is well known, cf. *shumâti = shuâti*, etc. This is due, of course, to the fact that the *m* was sounded like *w*.

established, cf. *inûḫ* from *inawuḫ*, *imtût* from *imtawut*, etc.[1] The Babylonian *ûru ûrru* is doubtless the same word. The fact that אורשלם is written *Ursalimmu* in cuneiform, and the West Semitic name אורמלך is written *Uru-milki*, etc., make it quite probable that the name was read *Ûru* or *Ûrru*. This is the way the Talmudic form אוריא, which is the late form of *Amurrû*, is read (see below). This being granted, it is possible to conclude that the word written *Amurru* and *Amuru*, which represents the *'Amôr* of the West, was pronounced *Awuru* by the late Babylonians, and that this became *Ûru*. In other words, we have the formula *Amurrû* = *Ûrru* or *Ûru*.

The question arises, can this be said to hold true also for the early period? In the early inscriptions there are several words written with *w* which have *m* in the later period. This rests entirely upon the reading of the character *PI* as having the values *wa, wi, wu,* and *we*. Formerly the sign was read with the values *ma, mi, mu, me,* etc. The stems or words which occur in the early period that show this change are *awêlu, awâtu, ḫâwiru, nawâru,* and a verbal form *uwaeiranni*. It is, therefore, maintained that the stems originally contained *w*, which later became *m*. This necessitates the assumption that the change from *w* to *m* had already taken place in the Hammurabi period, for in the contract literature, which more clearly represents the spoken language, such names

---

[1] Cf. Delitzsch, *Assyrische Grammatik*, p. 118; Ungnad, *Babylonisch assyrische Grammatik*, p. 47; and Meissner, *Assyrische Grammatik*, p. 51.

are found as *Namratum*, which is considered to belong to the stem *nawâru*;[1] *Shamash-li-wi-ir*, the father of *Ibgatum*, written *Shamash-li-me-ri*,[2] and *A-wi-ir-tum*, written *A-me-ir-rum*.[3] In the Cassite period, with the exception of an example like *A-wi-lu-tum*,[4] these words, as far as they occur, have *m*.

This change of consonant is in reversed order from that of the late period. Considering also that initial *w* of the early period, as in *warad*, etc., is dropped and also *w* is dropped between two vowels, as in *ḫîrtu*, *iḫîr* from *ḫawâru*, and that there is practically no support from the cognate languages for the view that *w* is original in these stems, except the late Aramaic הוא, which it is claimed is the stem of *awâtu*, it seems as if the last word has not been written on the subject. Moreover, if in the late period the *m* of *Amurru*, *amêlu*, and perhaps *amâtu* was pronounced like *w*; and *amêlu*, *amâtu*, and the other words contained *w* in the early period, it is not improbable that Amurru was also pronounced Awurru in the early period. Yet it must be admitted that the absolute proof of the identification of *amûr* with *ûru* in the early Babylonian period, as well as in the West Semitic inscriptions, has not yet been furnished.

It is very inviting to suggest that perhaps this change of consonants was due to dialectical differences in the languages from the West, of which all traces are lost.

---

[1] See Ungnad, *B. A.*, VI, 5, p. 127.
[2] See Ranke, *P. N.*, p. 145.
[3] See Poebel, *B. E.*, VI, pl. 2, 4: 1, 12, 16, 22 and 8 : 14.
[4] See Clay, *B. E.*, XIV, 58 : 1.

This would obviate the necessity of assuming that the original and the later stems, nawâru and namâru, were both in use in the Hammurabi period; and this would also account for such synonyms as 'amâru and 'awâru.[1] On this supposition the identification of the West Semitic stem from which the word "Amorite" comes with אור, would become reasonable. However, while the other considerations seem to support the view that the differences are dialectical, and it would throw much welcome light on the subject, it is here offered only as a plausible conjecture.

The word for "West, sunset," etc., in the Babylonian Talmud is 'Ûrya (אוריא) = Awurrû = Amurrû.[2] In this connection we are reminded of the Talmudic 'Ûr (אור), "sunset, twilight, evening," and even 'Ûrta' (אורתא), "night," and the difficulty the Jews in Babylonia experienced in trying to understand how 'Ûr (אור), which ordinarily means "light," in this connection meant "darkness" or "the West." In the Babylonian Talmud the question is asked, "Why is the West called 'Ûrya? (אוריה, variant אור)," and the answer was because it means divine air (variant, light), meaning Palestine.[3] In other words, they did not appreciate the

---

[1] See Delitzsch, *Prologomena*, p. 28; and Halévy, in Muss-Arnolt, *Assyrian Dictionary*, p. 52. The fact that among the values of the cuneiform *MASH*, we find amâru and amîri (perhaps the same as Amîr, "summit," in Hebrew) alongside of shamshu, ellu, ibbu, namaru, etc., seems to support the view of these scholars that 'amâru and 'awâru are synonyms.

[2] See Meissner, *Supplement*, p. 10.

[3] See Jastrow, *Talmudic Dictionary*, p. 34.

origin of the term. While 'Ur (אוּר), the name of the country, means "light," to the Semite living in the East, i.e., Babylonia, it also meant "evening, darkness, West," etc.,[1] because *Amurru* or *Uru* was the land of the West, or of the sunset, i.e., the land of the "going in of the sun."

OTHER NAMES OF AMAR.

The chief arguments for the view that the movement was eastward into Babylonia are to be found in the fact that the culture of the Amorites was carried into that land. This, as we have seen, shows itself in such legends as Marduk-Tiamtu, Gilgamesh, etc., but especially in the worship of the great solar deity or deities of the West by the Babylonians. Besides the names *Amar* or *Mar* and *Amur*, already discussed, the following variant forms of the name of this same deity, considered in connection with the theory concerning the way they arose, strengthens the thesis here maintained.

---

[1] אֻרִים of Isaiah 24 : 15, is usually translated, "region of light," "East," cf. Buhl-Gesenius, *Hebrew Dictionary*. It is quite natural to assume that the word אוּר in Palestine should mean "East," i.e., the place of the rising of the light, and especially by reason of an antithesis with the word "isles," which were in the West. However, as קֶדֶם is the usual word for "East," and the word in question means "West" in Aramaic, it is quite probable that the meaning is the same in Hebrew. It must be noticed that the phrase which follows, referring to the "isles of the sea," can just as well be understood as being parallel, which would require the meaning "West."

URU.

A name of the solar deity of the West, as mentioned above, was *Ûru*. This name appeared in a number of variations, due to the different characters employed in writing it. In considering them it is necessary constantly to bear in mind that in representing Semitic words the Sumerian scribes employed ideograms irrespective of their value in the Sumerian language. For example, there were a number of different signs, meaning respectively "city," "dwelling," "servant," etc., all of which were pronounced *URU*. In writing this name of the god of the Semitic hordes that came from the West, the Sumerians used these and other signs which were pronounced exactly the same as the name of the deity.

In Ranke's work, *Personal Names of the Hammurabi Dynasty*, there are a large number of names compounded with the deity *Urra*, the god of Cutha, who is identified with Nergal. In the tablets of the Ur and Nisin dynasties, no less than fourteen different names are compounded with this element *Urra* (written *NITA*, which has the value *ur*, see below, with the phonetic complement *ra*).[1] In the name of the founder of the Isin

---

[1] See Huber, *Personennamen aus der Zeit der Könige von Ur und Nisin*, who reads *Urú-ra*. Although he places the element in the list of deities, he reads *ardu*, and translates "servant." Cf. *ibid.*, p. 170. Ranke, *ibid.*, p. 208, has shown that the character *NITA* also had the value *ur*. This element is, therefore, to be read *Ur-ra*, and the names are to be read *Urra-bâni*, "Ur is creator"; *Urra-BA-TIL*, "Ur has given life," etc.

110 AMURRU HOME OF NORTHERN SEMITES

dynasty, *Ishbi-Urra*, both elements seem to be West Semitic.[1]

In these same texts there is also a deity *Uru* or *Ur*, written *NITA* without the phonetic complement *ra*, and also *USH*.[2] Here should be mentioned also the name *NITA*(or *GIR*)-*A-MU*,[3] which probably is to be read *Ûra(a)-iddin*, "*Ûra* has given," or *Ûra-apil-iddin*, "*Ûra* gave a son," unless *MU* in the early period does not have the value *nadanu*.

This discussion throws additional light upon the king's name now generally read *Warad-Sin* or *Arad-Sin*, and identified by some with Arioch of the fourteenth chapter of Genesis. The identification is highly plausible, because *Warad-Sin* was the king of Larsa, which city

---

[1] *Ishbi* is a Babylonianized form of a West Semitic element, cf. *Ja-ash-bi-i-la*, found in Ranke, *Personal Names*, p. 144. ישבו of 2 Samuel 21 : 16, may also represent the element.

[2] Huber, *Personennamen*, p. 57, note 1, grouped these together, and says = *ardu*, "servant." *URU-DINGIR-RA* translated *Arad-ili*, "servant of god," makes sense, but something seems to be wrong with the common *URU-MU* (= *URU-iddin*), if translated "a servant has given"; or *URU-LIG-GA*, which Huber, feeling that *ardu* cannot be correct, translates "The strong *URU*." Further, such names as *GAL(Amêlu)-URU*, "man of servant," *GIR-URU*, "slave of servant," and *DUMU-URU*, "son of servant," would give strange meanings if *URU* were translated "Knecht." Huber appreciated this, and added that "In many names *URU* = *URU-RA* seems to have been used as an equivalent for a god's name, or, he asks, is it a synonym of *abdu*, "servant"? Unquestionably we have here also the name of the god *Ûru*, and the names mean "*Uru* has given," "*Uru* is mighty," "servant of *Ûru*" and "the son of *Ûru*."

[3] Scheil, *Manishtusu*, D. 5 : 2.

is identical with Ellasar of the Old Testament, over which Arioch ruled. He was also a cotemporary of Amraphel,[1] the Hammurabi of the inscriptions, and his father, Kudur-Mabug, the king of Emutbal, or Elam, was king of Syria and Palestine at this particular time, which is in strict accordance with Genesis, where we learn that Elam was the suzerain power in that land. The identification is based especially upon the fact that the second element of the name can be read *Aku* as well as *Sin*, and that the first character, read *Ardu*, has also the dialectical value *Eri*.

These facts, which are well known, have been accepted by a large number of scholars, but some seem to exercise more than ordinary critical caution with reference to the identification. In the first place, the name list of the Isin and Ur dynasties show that *Aku* or *Agu* was frequently used in personal names.[2] Further, in these Sumerian centers it cannot be shown by phonetically written examples that the element was read *Wardu* or *Ardu* in the early period. In all probability it was read *Ur* or *Eri*. Where the element is followed by the name of a god, although another translation is possible, namely, "*Uru* is *Aku*," we would naturally translate "servant of *Aku*." At the same time, the fact that

---

[1] Since the appearance of my *Light on the Old Testament from Babel*, Thureau-Dangin has shown that *Warad-Sin* and *Rim-Sin* were two personages, both being sons of Kudur-Mabug.

[2] See Huber, *Personennamen*, p. 167; also cf. *A-ku-i-lum* and *A-ku-Ea* of the Manishtusu Obelisk.

112 AMURRU HOME OF NORTHERN SEMITES

there is an Elamite deity *Eria*[1] must not be lost sight of, and especially as the king's father, Kudur-Mabug, was ruler over Emutbal, a name of or part of Elam. Moreover, it seems to me that the only conclusion at which we can arrive is, that the ruler's name was not pronounced *Arad-Sin*, but *Uri(or Eri)-Aku*.

Two other ideograms which have the reading *Ûru* are found in names of the early period, *Ûri(BUR-BUR)-DA*[2] and *Ûru-DA*.[3] Huber[4] says "*Uru* = the holy city, a god's name(?).'' While I question the reading *âlu*, "city," it must be recalled that there is a deity or epithet, *A-li*, frequently found in the names of the First dynasty, *e.g.*, *A-li-ba-ni-shu*, " Ali is his creator," etc.,[5] and also that the name of a deity often appears as substitutes for the patron deity in names. Very probably, however, we have here also the name of the deity *Ûru*. With this understanding the above names make sense.

The names of the early kings, *Ûru-MU-USH*[6] and

---

[1] See Hinke, *Nebuchadrezzar I*, p. 222.
[2] See *Cuneiform Texts*, X, 24, 14,313, Ob. 1.
[3] *ÛRU* in the latter means "city" in Sumerian. Huber, *Personennamen*, p. 56, reads the name *Itti-ali*(?), "with a city." Also *Uru(URU)-MU*, he reads *âlu-iddin*, which translated would be "the city has given." *Uru(URU)-ki-bi* he translates "Die Stadt spricht"; *Uru(URU)-KA-GI-NA* he translates "Die Stadt verstummt(?)"; *Uru(URU)-NI-BA-AGA*, "Seine Stadt ist Liebling;" *Uru(URU)-BA-SAG-SAG = âlu-udammiq*, etc.
[4] Cf. *ibid.*, p. 189.
[5] See lists in Ranke, *Personal Names*, his B. E., vol. VI, pt. 1, and Poebel, B. E., vol. VI, pt. 2.
[6] Perhaps *mush* is Semitic, cf. מוש, etc., of the Old Testament. King, *Proceedings of Society of Biblical Archaeology*, vol. XXX, 1908, p. 239, suggests the reading *Rí-mu-ush*.

Uru-KA-GI-NA, which would be equivalent to the Semitic Ikûn-pî-Uru, "true or established is the word of Uru," receive new light.[1] This reading of URU = Uru may also throw welcome light on the title of Sargon, namely, shar-URU, hitherto considered part of the name and read Shargani-shar-âli, and more recently Shar-Gani-sharri (see Appendix on "The Name of Sargon").

This discovery of additional forms under which the god Uru occurs by no means exhausts the occurrences of the name in the early literature, it being the purpose to give simply the various writings of the name; but from these considerations we are forced to recognize the prominence of this deity Uru in the early period.

In the early Sumerian and Semitic inscriptions, therefore, the name is written UR-RA, UR-A, NITA (more correctly UR), USH (perhaps better URU), URU (âlu), BUR-BUR (= Uri), KUR-GAL (= Uru),[2] URU (shubtu), see below, and BIL-LIL, see below, all of which = Uru, Uri, Ura or Urra; and perhaps also MAR-TU (= Uru).

This solar deity throughout the early period must have been recognized as foreign, because until the time of Hammurabi it did not, as Ranke[3] has noted, have the determinative for god.[4] Just as the scribe of the

---

[1] For similar names, see Ranke, *Personal Names*.

[2] If the name Uru-KA-GI-NA of the early ruler of Shirpurla contains the name Uru, it is possible also that A-KUR-GAL, of the same dynasty, contains the name or an epithet of the same deity.

[3] *Personal Names*, p. 208.

[4] There are, however, exceptions, as GAL-^{d}UR-RA, Reissner, *Urkunden*, 94, I, 35.

114 AMURRU HOME OF NORTHERN SEMITES

Cassite documents at Nippur, as a rule, did not prefix the determinative to the names of the Cassite deities (with the exception of *Shuqamuna*, who had been introduced into the Babylonian pantheon) in the same way, the Sumerian scribes in the early period probably regarded this god of the Amorites as foreign. This, it seems to be evident, was done because of the religious prejudices of the scribes. And yet it must be borne in mind that such deities as Sin or Nannar in this as well as the earlier period are frequently written without the determinative. The Legend of *Urra*, which echoes severe conflicts waged against certain Babylonian cities by some rival power, also points to a foreign district over which the god presided.

It may be of interest to add that the earliest inscribed object dedicated to the god *Urra*, is a vase which is in the Morgan Library Collection. It is dedicated by or for a son of Lugal-kisalsi, who belongs perhaps to the fourth millennium B. C.[1] The name of the god is written *DINGIR BIL-LIL*, which, according to Rawlinson, IV, 5, 66a, is to be read *Urra*.

NERGAL.

Nergal, the patron deity of Cutha, is also a solar deity,[2] who in the late period is the god of the burning heat of the sun, or the god of the all-destroying midday

---

[1] See Banks, "A Vase Inscription from Warka," *American Journal of Semitic Languages*, XXI, p. 63.

[2] See Jensen, *Kosmologie*, p. 484 f.; Zimmern, *K. A. T.*³, p. 412, and Jastrow, *Rel. Bab. und Ass.*, p. 157.

sun. The great heat of the sun in Babylonia has a highly destructive power, which doubtless gave rise to the attributes attached to this deity when he became the god of pestilence, death and the underworld.[1] One of the Sumerian ideograms for the deity is *NE-URU-GAL*, which gave rise to the familiar *Nergal*. Scholars have considered this ideogram to mean "Lord of the great dwelling" (*i.e.*, Hades). Haupt, following Delitzsch,[2] and others have thus regarded it.[3] In the light of these investigations, there can be little doubt that this sign *URU*, which ordinarily has the meaning "dwelling," was selected by the Sumerian scribes at Cutha, as mentioned above, simply because it represented the sound *Ûru*. The last two elements of the name would then mean "great *Ûru*." The name of the god is frequently found written in this abbreviated form, as *U-ri-gal-la*,[4] *Urra-gal*, etc. Further, the first element *NE*[5] does not seem to mean "lord,"[6] but *nûru*, "light,"[7] although it should be borne in mind that the meaning "Lord *Ûru*," if *NE* is translated "lord," would be parallel to "King *Ûru*" (*i.e.*, *LUGAL-URU*), another name of this deity. The name then of this Amorite

---

[1] See Jensen, *Kosmologie*, pp. 476–487.

[2] *American Journal of Philology*, VIII, p. 274, and *Proceedings of American Oriental Society*, October, 1887, XI.

[3] See also Zimmern, *K. A. T.*,[3] p. 412.

[4] Strassmaier, *Nbk.* 305 : 4.

[5] In the Naram-Sin inscription found in Susa a deity *NIN-NÊ-URU(UNU)* occurs, cf. Thureau-Dangin, *Vor. Bib.*, I, p. 168.

[6] The sign, however, has the value *gashru*; cf. Brünnow, *List.*

[7] Cf. Meissner, *Seltene Ideogramme*, No. 6920.

sun-god, when written by the Sumerian scribes at Cutha, meant "The light of the great *Uru,*" or perhaps "Lord Urugal."

The deity *ᵈLUGAL-URU* has also been identified with Nergal, as above. In a passage from Rawlinson, *Inscriptions of Western Asia,*[1] we seem to have proof that this deity is from *Amurru.* It reads: *ᵈShar-ra-pu = DINGIR LUGAL-UR-RA MAR-KI,* i.e., "The deity *Sharrapu* (the burner) = *Lugal-Urra* (Lord *Uru*) of *Amurru.*"[2]

MARDUK.

Another striking proof of the transmission is to be seen in the name of the god *Marduk,* whose solar character is attested by Berosus, which was first pointed out by Sayce.[3] After Hammurabi placed this god of light at the head of the pantheon, and made him supplant the other gods, his solar features were overshadowed by the many other attributes with which he was invested, and as a consequence they were more or less lost sight of.

The deity under the name *Marduk* is not known in the Hebrew of the early period, and with one exception, i.e., *DI-Marduk,* the name does not occur in the Amarna letters. This is significant, and shows, as stated (p. 36), that the supposed great influence exerted by Babylonian

---

[1] V, 46c–d, 22.
[2] Cf. *K. A. T.*³, p. 415, note I.
[3] *Trans. Soc. Bib. Arch.,* 1893, II, p. 246; cf. also Jensen, *Kosmologie,* p. 88.

culture upon the West is more or less a myth, since this deity, who was at the head of the Babylonian pantheon for more than a half millennium prior to the Amarna period, the god that Hammurabi made supplant Ellil, lord of lands, and to whom was given the attributes of the other gods, is scarcely known by that name in Palestine and Syria. Hence it follows that the original name of the god, if indigenous in the West, must have been different; in which case it is reasonable to inquire whether the deity cannot be *DINGIR-MARTU*, the deity of *Amurru*, perhaps also known as *Ûru*. In this connection the personal name *U-ri-Marduk*, "*Uri* is *Marduk*," of the Cassite period, is most interesting,[1] but especially the formula *AMAR-UTU* = ^{d}A-*ma-ru*.[2]

The Sumerian scribes in Babylonia wrote the name of this deity *AMAR-UTU* or *AMAR-UTUG*. Some scholars have proposed, in order to account for the writing *Marduk* or *Maruduk*, that the second character is to be read *UTUG*. This is quite reasonable, for there is a sign having the value *U-tu-ki*, which also means the god Shamash (^{d}UTU).[3] *UTU* may have the value

---

[1] See Clay, *B. E.*, vol. XV, p. 45.

[2] Cf. Brünnow, *List* 11,566. This is equivalent to *Avaru* = אור = *Ûru*. Cf. here also *LUGAL-UDDA*, quoted as an epithet of *Marduk* by Jensen, *K. B.*, VI, 562. Of course, *UDDA* has also the value *ûru*. Now *LUGAL-URRU* is another name of *Nergal* (see above), in which case we have direct evidence of the connection between *Nergal* and *Marduk*.

[3] See Brünnow, *List*, No. 12,219.

utuk, for it is well known that a final *G*, including the vowel, in Sumerian is often apocopated.[1]

Jensen explains *AMAR-UT* to mean "the son of the sun."[2] This explanation, however, is based on a fragment of questionable value. Pinches'[3] explains *AMAR-UDUG* to mean "the brightness of the day." Hommel[4] considers *AMAR* to mean "young wild ox," which explanation he feels is confirmed by one of the dates of *Bur-Sin*, where his name is written *Amar-Sin*.[5] Sayce[6] explains the name as having a punning etymology, *Amar-utuk*, "heifer of the goblin."

It is possible to understand how a deity like Marduk could have an epithet, "Son of Shamash;" but it does not seem appropriate to explain the name of the patron deity of Babylon in that way. And notwithstanding

---

[1] See Leander, *Sumerische Lehnwörter*, p. 34.

[2] Cf. K. B., VI, p. 562. "*AMAR-UT-mar* = *pŭru* = 'Junges'-*māri-shamashu*, d. i. ein 'Sonnenkind' oder 'Sonnensohn' der Götter, aber nicht 'Sonne' schlechthin."

[3] *Old Testament in the Light of the Historical Inscriptions*, etc., p. 54.

[4] *Sumerian Lesestücke*, p. 51.

[5] It is quite evident that the names of both, the son of Dungi of the Ur dynasty, and the son of Ur-NIN-IB of the Isin, are not to be read *Bur-Sin;* and designated, as is usually done, *Bur-Sin I*, and *Bur-Sin II*. In every instance where the former occurs, the sign *AMAR* is written, cf. *C.T.*, XXI, 24, 25, 27, and Hilprecht, B.E., I, pt. 1, 20, 22, XX, 47 : 3, etc., whereas the latter name is written with *BUR*, cf. B. E., I, pt. 1, 19, and XX, 47 : 15. Moreover in B. E., XX : 47, both names appear. Until, therefore, a phonetic writing is found, although *AMAR* may be read *Bur*, the reading *Amar-Sin* for the former and *Bur-Sin* for the latter is preferable.

[6] *Religion of Egypt and Babylonia*, p. 325.

the other explanations, it does not seem out of place to offer still other conjectures.

If *Amar* is a synonym of אור, "light," as has been suggested, which Pinches apparently had in mind in translating "brightness," then the first element of the name could also be a synonym of *NE* (= *nûru*), which is found in *NE-URU-GAL*, "Light of the great *Ûru*," and also of *SIR* (= *nûru* or *napâḫu*) in *SIR*-(usually read *BU)NE-NE*, "Light or flame of the fire," the charioteer of Shamash of Sippar. In this case *AMAR-UTUG* would mean "Light of *Utuk*," i.e., the sun. *A-ma-ru*, which, as we saw above, is equivalent to *Marduk*, would then represent perhaps only the first element. This would mean, if correct, that in writing this name the Amorite element *Amar* was used in connection with the Sumerian *UTUG* or the Babylonized *utuk*.

Another explanation is perhaps more plausible. Words were compounded in Babylonian in other than the Semitic construct relation.[1] Many of these compositions doubtless arose through the influence of Sumerian writing.[2]

---

[1] See Delitzsch, *Assyrische Grammatik*.

[2] In this connection I desire to call attention to several names of woods, stones, animals and plants, some of which may eventually be shown to be similar in formation. The name of the country Amurru, being the same as the deity, among the many variations in form in which the name appears we have *Amar*, *Mar*, *Amur*, *Mur*, *Ur* and *Ar*.

Plants: *A-mur-tin-nu* (II R., 45, 58); *A-mur-ri-qa-nu* (also a sickness of the eye, cf. Arabic *araq* and *uraq*, "grain sickness");

120 AMURRU HOME OF NORTHERN SEMITES

As is customary at the present time to designate the origin of animals, woods, etc., by mentioning the name of the country, as, for example, "Scotch terrier," "Italian marble," etc., it seems natural to postulate that the Babylonians did the same in naming foreign materials. And this being the case, Amurru should figure prominently in that respect, for frequently we read in the inscriptions, as early as the time of Gudea, that this land was the forest that furnished woods for their temples, and the quarry where they got certain kinds of stone. *Amar-utuk* may, therefore, mean "the Amorite *Utuk*," *i.e.*, "the Amorite sun-god." One other explanation seems probable and worth considering.

AMAR-UTUG, being an Amorite deity, contains as its first element *Amar*, meaning the deity (see above). In the light of these considerations, therefore, is it not reasonable to suggest that the name means "*Amar*

Awa-ar-ka-ṣir (II R., 43 : 67a and b); *Awa-ar-si-qir* (*ibid.*); *Awa-ar-sa-na-bu* (Delitzsch, *H. W. B.*, p. 51), etc. Woods: *Ur-ḫa-lu-ub* (*Vor. Bib.*, I, pp. 30, 96) seems to belong to *Amurru*; *Ur-karinnu* (Esarhaddon, I : 20) is brought with cedar from Sidon; *Mar-eriqqu* (Muss-Arnolt, *Dic.*, 4148), etc. Stones: *Mur-ar-na-tim* (Brünnow, 12803); *Mur-siparru* (Brünnow, 13279); *Ar-gaman*, which is Phœnician dye. גוון in Syriac means "color," etc. Animals: *A-mur-sa-nu*; *A-mur-si-gu* (Meissner, *Supplement*, p. 5); *Awa-ar-i-lum* (= *Mur-babillu*, Muss-Arnolt, *Dic.*, p. 90, and Delitzsch, *H. W. B.*, p. 51); *Mur-nisqi* (Muss-Arnolt, *Dic.*, p. 584, root *nasâqu*), etc.

These words, the etymology of nearly all of which is in doubt, taken from a fuller list, I simply offer in order to raise the question whether some of them at least cannot be explained as containing perhaps the element discussed, and especially as we have similar formations, as *ashar-edu*, perhaps arisen from the Sumerian.

is *Utuk,*" or the "*Amar-Utuk,*" like Bêl-Marduk, El-Shaddai, Bir-Hadad, Yahweh-Sebaoth? This being true, the Sumerian scribes, perhaps, in this way differentiated in writing the name of the sun-god of the Semites from their own solar deity, *UTU* or *UTUG*.

Moreover, even though none of these conjectures shall eventually prove to be correct, it does seem that the first element *AMAR* represents the name or epithet of the chief deity of the Amorites.

NIN-IB.

NIN-IB, who so frequently interchanges with Nergal, is also a Babylonian solar deity that was imported from the West; or, to express it differently, the name represents another writing of the Amoritic sun-god.[1] The Aramaic equivalent which the writer published several years ago, namely, אנשת, and which he consistently maintained was correctly read against the views of others, has recently been placed beyond doubt by the discovery of Professor Montgomery of the name written on an ostracon no less than five times (see Appendix). This Aramaic equivalent has received thus far about fifteen different explanations. The writer, however, feels that the one he recently offered,' namely, אנשת = *EN-MASHTU* for *EN-MAR-TU,* which is Sumerian for *bêl Amurru,* "Lord of Amurru or Uru," like *LUGAL-Ûru,* which has practically the same

---

[1] See Clay, "The Origin and Real Name of *NIN-IB,*" *Journal of American Oriental Society,* vol. XXVIII, 1907; also the Appendix on "The Name of *NIN-IB.*"

meaning, has not been improved upon. There is, however, another plausible explanation of this name, which may eventually be found to be correct.

We have seen in Part I that the mountain *Mâshu* figures prominently in the Gilgamesh epic, and that it is located in the land of Amurru. We have further seen how in the name *Gilga-mesh* and in the names of several temples in Babylonia the element *Mash* or *Mesh* figures, and that this element in all probability is foreign. Now, as is well known, another common ideogram for *NIN-IB* is *MASH*. The first element *NIN* meaning "Lady or Mistress," and the name *NIN-IB*, "Lady *IB*," who was the consort of the god *IB*, shows that originally the deity was feminine. As there was a West Semitic deity called *Mash*, his consort should be called *Mashtu*. In Babylonian, there is a deity *Mash* and also his consort *Mashtu*. Knowing as we do that this deity, like Nin-Girsu and others, became masculinized, it is altogether reasonable to assume that even in early times the deity became *EN-Mashtu*, that is, "Lord Mashtu." This as well as the above explanation identifies the deity with the West, which is further discussed, and for which additional proofs are given in the Appendix on "The Name *NIN-IB*."

URASH.

The god *Urash*, written *IB* and perhaps also *IB-BA*,[1] who was the local deity of Dilbat, is doubtless also a

---

[1] See Clay, *B. E.*, vol. XIV, p. 59.

solar deity from Amurru. This follows from the determination of *NIN-IB*, who was originally the consort of *IB*, as being Amorite.

It occurs in *Ebed-Urash* in the Amarna letters. Now in a Punic inscription of the third century B.C. there occurs the name עבד־ארש, which in all probability is the same; compare also טבארשא.[1] *Urash* may be a contraction of אר־אש, *Ur-esh*, i.e., *Ûru-Esh*, like *Bir-Adad* or *Amar-Utuk*, etc. (see above). The first element in Esh-ba‘al (אשבעל), son of Saul, and Ashbel (אשבל, Ιασβηλ), the name of a son of Benjamin (Gen. 46 : 21), may of course be א״ש, "man," but I prefer to see in it the deity *Esh*, "fire-god"; compare *Ishum* especially in the Hammurabi period.[2] *IB=Urash* has the value *aqmu*,[3] perhaps "I burned," and considering that *IB* is the consort of *NIN-IB*, a solar deity, the above explanation seems at least plausible.[4]

SHAMASH.

Shamash, whose temple was at Sippar, is naturally recognized as the great solar deity of the Babylonian Semites. At the same time, we have only to recall the fact that in the Amarna letters Shamash is the one all-

---

[1] Cooke, *North Semitic Inscriptions*, p. 70, compares the root ארש, which in Assyrian (*erêshu*) = "desire, request," and the Hebrew ארשת; but *ibid.*, p. 129, in discussing עבדארש, he thinks it is a deity, and compares Ἄρης.

[2] See Ranke, *Personal Names*.

[3] See Brünnow, *List* No. 10481.

[4] For another explanation of *Urash* see Dhorme, *O. L. Z.*, 1909.

important deity, so frequently named in the salutation. The Pharaoh addressed is called "my Shamash, my god (*ilî*,[1] *i.e.*, *pluralis intensivus*), my lord." These three terms correspond to the Hebrew Yahweh, Elohim, "god," and Adonai, "lord." It is not impossible that the Egyptian sun-god Rê, or the foreign importation Aten was meant, who the Egyptians believed was incarnated in the Pharaoh; but if that were true, we would expect at least a single variant, in which one or the other was referred to by that name. It is more probable that the Amorite writer meant his own sun-deity which he associated with the deity of the

---

[1] In spite of the pronounced views of others who have differed with the explanations offered for *DINGIR-DINGIR* or *DINGIR MESH* = Elohim (אלהים), the generic name of the god among the Hebrews and the people of the West (cf. Hilprecht, Editorial Preface to my *B. E.*, vol. X, p. IX), I continue to maintain that this explanation offered by Barton (*Proc. Amer. Orien. Soc.*, April, 1892) is in all probability correct. That *DINGIR-MESH* = אל, in the names of the Achæmenian period, I have conclusively shown in my paper on Aramaic Endorsements in the Harper *Memorial Volume* (I, p. 287 ff.). Unless it can be proved that the word Elohim of the Old Testament was not in use as early as the second millennium B.C., there is every reason to expect to find it in the literature of Palestine, and especially in the Amarna letters. This being true, there are good reasons for believing that in the name *Warad-DINGIR-DINGIR-MAR-TU* we must recognize the generic name for "God" used by the Western Semites; that is, instead of translating "gods of Amurru," the writer believes that in the early period, as well as in the late, the scribes differentiated between *ilu* and אל or אלהים. Moreover, a modification of this view might be suggested, which is that the name was probably read *Warad-El-Ûru*. Considered in connection with אלור in the Pognon inscription, this explanation appears reasonable.

Egyptian, which he knew was also solar. Without taking into consideration place names, such as Beth-Shemesh, etc., or perhaps names as Samson (*Shimshôn*) in Palestine, it must be acknowledged that the Amorites and Aramæans used extensively the name Shamash or Shemesh for their chief deity. Not only the Amarna letters show this, but also the so-called Cappadocian tablets published by Sayce, Delitzsch and Pinches.

The Sumerian chirographers, in writing the name Shamash at Sippar, used the same ideogram *UTU* which stood for their own solar deity, whose seat of worship was at Larsa. That the Semitic name Shamash prevailed in that city is an indication that the deity in his original habitat was known under that name.

No satisfactory etymology of the name Shamash has yet been offered. The idea that it is derived from a stem שמש, which in Aramaic means "to minister unto, to serve," because in the Babylonian pantheon Shamash is the son of Nannar or Sin, and occupies a subservient position to the moon-god, does not appear plausible. The reason why the god Sin is accorded a superior rank must be due to other influences and to the fact that Shamash is foreign. The all-powerful element of the universe certainly would not represent a deity subsidiary to the moon in his own habitat. The only reasonable explanation for the position which Shamash occupies in the pantheon, especially when we recall that most of the deities of the Semitic Babylonians are solar, is that the moon-god cult of such cities as Ur and Haran was able to establish its deity in the foremost position during the rule of some powerful dynasty.[1] Besides this Aramaic stem, which has led scholars to give the meaning "servitor" to Shamash, no other seems to exist from which the name can be derived. Taking this into consideration, the following is offered as a plausible conjecture.

The name *Mash*, more than has been realized, figures prominently in the Eastern as well as in the Western Semitic cultures. *Mash* in the Old Testament is called one of the sons of Aram (Gen. 10 : 23). *Mâshu* is the mountain where the gates of the setting sun were found. This, as has been stated (p. 77), is probably to be located in Amurru and perhaps is Hermon, near Damascus (see below).

This element *Mash* is frequently met with in the Babylonian inscriptions. It occurs in a number of temple names, for example *E-UL-MASH*, *E-MASH-MASH*, *E-MESH-LAM*, etc. It is also found in the name *Gilga-Mesh* (see p. 78). This solar hero was associated with Erech, where a deity *Mesh* was worshiped.[2] The name of the solar deity *Lugal-Urra* or Nergal is written with the signs *MASH-MASH*. This deity is of Western origin. The name *NIN-IB*, another of the chief solar deities of Babylonia, is written in cuneiform $^{d}MASH$, and is phonetically written *Ma-a-shu* in a

---

[1] Prof. Jastrow, *Rel. Bab. und Ass.*, II, p. 457, maintains that astrological considerations are responsible for the relative positions of Sin and Shamash.

[2] Cf. *Collection de Clerq*, IX : 82.

syllabary.[1] *NIN-IB*, while prominently worshiped in Babylonia, is also a deity of the West. In Aramaic the name is written אנושת=*EN-Mâshtu*,[2] *i.e.*, "Lord *Mâshtu*." *Mâshtu* is known in cuneiform, and is perhaps to be identified with *Vashti* of the Book of Esther. The gods *Mâshu* and *Mâshtu* are called the children of Sin.[3] *Shamash* was also regarded as the offspring of Sin.[4] The sign *MASH*, it may be mentioned also, has such values as *shamshu, ellu, ibbu, amâru, namâru*, etc.

The deity whose habitat was found in the mountain *Mash* might well be called, following the Semitic usage with a relative particle, *Sha-Mash*, or *El Shammash*, *i.e.*, "He of Mash," or "The god of Mash." This has its parallel in Babylonian where "Man of sealing" or "of the seal," is written *hshakkanaku*.[5] The relative is commonly found as an element in Babylonian personal names, *e.g.*, *Sha-Addu*, etc.[6] It is also found in the West Semitic names *Methû-shā-El* and *Mî-shā-El*. *Bêth-sha-El* (written *Bayt-sha-ra*),[7] one of the frequently mentioned cities of Palestine in the Egyptian inscriptions, also seems to

---

[1] Cf. Brünnow, List No. 1778.
[2] See Appendix on the name NIN-IB.
[3] See Appendix on the name NIN-IB.
[4] See Jastrow, *Rel. of Bab. and Ass.*, p. 68.
[5] Cf. also *hshangu* "man of sacrifice," and *hshabru* "man of seeing."
[6] See Tallqvist, *Neubabylonisches Namenbuch*, p. 331, and Ranke, *P. N.*, p. 245. If this explanation of the name *Shamash* should prove correct, it is not impossible that *El Shaddai* is a similar formation, perhaps containing the element *Addu*.
[7] See W. M. Müller, *Europa und Asien*, p. 192, and *Mitteilungen der vorderasiat. Gesellschaft*, XII, 1907, 29.

128 AMURRU HOME OF NORTHERN SEMITES

contain the particle. It probably represents the city Bethel.[1] The relative is also found in Arabic divine names, e.g., Dhû'l Ḥalaṣa, Dhu'l Sharâ, etc.,[2] and also in Old South Arabic names, e.g., Dhû Samâwi.[3] The explanation that Shamash contains the relative would give a reason for the doubling of m in Il-Tammesh,[4] for, as is well known, one of the forms of the particle doubles the following consonant. As stated above, this is offered simply as a conjecture in the absence of any reasonable explanation of Shamash.

A word may properly be added here with reference to the name Damascus. The fact that it is a very ancient and important city raises the question whether it is not mentioned in the early Babylonian inscriptions.

It seems that Damascus must be Qi-Mash-qi which figures so prominently in the inscriptions of Gudea and Dungi. This city is usually considered to be in Arabia,[5] but the scene of Dungi's operations were chiefly in Amurru. In the absence of any proof that KI or QI is Semitic, this would mean that the name of the city as known in cuneiform was or became the name of the

---

[1] In Papyrus Anastasi I, -sha-êl occurs, which prompted scholars to think of Bethel instead of Bethshean.

[2] Wellhausen, Reste Arabischen Heidentumes, p. 42 ff.

[3] Baethgen, Beiträge, p. 123 f.

[4] There are a few variant forms as Il-Tamesh, Il-Temesh, see Tallqvist, Neubabylonisches Namenbuch, p. 288.

[5] Delitzsch (Paradies, p. 242 f.) has, however, made it quite reasonable that the desert of Syria is referred to in Ashurbanipal's campaign as the desert of Mash. Jensen now also places Mâshu in the Lebanon district.

AMURRU IN CUNEIFORM INSCRIPTIONS 129

city. In the inscription of Gudea *KA-GAL-AD-KI* is the mountain of *QI-MASH*, which is also called the "mountain of copper" (*ḪAR-SAG-URUDU-GE*). Perhaps the name means "gate" (*KA-GAL*) "of copper" (*AD?*); at least *AD-ḪAL* means copper. This idea of a gate reminds us of the gate of the setting sun in the Gilga-Mesh epic at the mountain *Mâshu*; and also the passage, Zech. 6:1, where it says the four chariots passed between the two mountains of brass. Damascus is east of Hermon and southeast of an offshoot of the Antilebanon, perhaps such a location where the idea of a gate of the setting sun, referred to in the Gilga-Mesh epic, would arise. It may be that the gate was formed by Mount Hermon and Mount Lebanon. But more important than all else is the fact that there were copper mines east of the Lebanon range in this land of *Nuḫashshi*[1] of the Amarna Letters. The city alongside of *Mash* would probably be called "City of Mash." This identification finds support in the passage, Gen. 15:2, where Eliezer is called בֶּן מֶשֶׁק, "Son of Mesheq."[2] The question then arises, how shall the first part of the name be understood?

The name of the city is written דַּרְמֶשֶׂק, דַּרְמֶשֶׁק and דּוּמֶשֶׂק in the Old Testament; *Ti-mas-qu, Sa-ra-mas-qi* (for *Ti-ra-mas-qi*) in Egyptian; *Ti-ma-ash-gi, Di-mash-qa* in the Amarna letters; *Di-ma-ash-qi, Di-*

---

[1] *Enc. Bib.*, II, col. 893.
[2] The words following are a gloss explaining in a later period that *Mesheq* is *Dammesheq*. The passage reads "a son of *Mesheq* is my family—that is Damascus—Eliezer."

9

mas-qa, Dim-mas-qa, etc., in the Assyrian inscriptions; and *Dimashqu*, etc., in Arabic. In view of the above explanation of *Sha-Mash*, and the doubling of the *m*[1] in the name, it is possible to see here the relative particle (see above). This view finds support in the other form of the name, *^{al}Sha-imeri-shu*.[2] If this should prove correct, then the early name Mesheq, perhaps arisen from the cuneiform writing of the name *Mash^{ai}*, later became *Dammesheq*, "(city) of Mesheq."

Another and more reasonable explanation is that the first element written *Dar, Dum* (for *Dur*), and even *Sara* in Egyptian, is equivalent to the Aramaic *Der* and the Babylonian *dûr*, "fortress," etc., which is doubtless from the Aramaic stem דור, "to enclose, or to surround," and continues in the late Aramaic dialect as

---

[1] The *r* in several of the forms could have been used for the dissimulation of *mm*.

[2] The other form of the name in cuneiform is *Sha-imeri-shu* (*Sha-i-me-ri-shu*, III R, 2, XX), *Sha-NITA-shu* and *Sha-NITA-MESH-shu* (III R. 9, 50). These writings can be reconciled if the second sign is read *amaru* (Brünnow, *List*, 4983), *i.e., Amar* the "god," instead of *imeru* the "ass," and *NITA* as *Ura*, perhaps *Mir* (Brünnow, *List*, Nos. 954 and 955). or *NITA-MESH* as *Mirî*. *SHU* (although in the late period another sign *SHU* is used) has the value *erêbu*, especially in connection with *shamshu* (cf. Brünnow, *List*, 10828), *AMAR* or *MIR-SHU* would then be equivalent to *MAR-TU*, or *erib shamshi*, "the setting sun." *Sha-AMAR-SHU* would mean "The city of the setting sun," a most appropriate name for Damascus. However, the fact that this would again bring the Semitic relative into connection with a Sumerian ideogram must be recognized as an objection, unless we assume that the cuneiform script was extensively used in that district in the third millennium B.C., and the ideogram had early become Semitized.

dûrû, "circuit, enclosure." The name would then mean circuit or enclosure or fortress of *Mesheq* (or *Mash*), instead of "Aselstadt." This has its parallel in the name Carchemish, which has been translated "Castle of Mish;" perhaps better, "Fortress Mash." The latter element is of course the name of the sun-god.

ADDU OR ADAD.

As is well known, *Addu* or *Ramman* in Babylonia appears as a god of rain and lightning, and in Syria, where he is indigenous, as shown by Jensen,[1] Jastrow,[2] Zimmern,[3] and others, he is recognized as a solar deity. This seems to have its parallel in Marduk[4] and in Nin-Girsu, the Sumerian sun-deity of Tello, who is also the god of agriculture. Naturally, the fructification and vivification of the earth is dependent upon the warmth of the sun together with the rain.

Addu is associated and identified with the god of the West, *i.e.*, *Amurru*. This seems to be well established;[5] *cf.* $MAR\text{-}TU = {}^{d}IM$ *sha abubê*, *i.e.*, "Addu of the floods." Compare the name in the Amarna letters *Amur-Adad* (${}^{d}IM$), *i.e.*, "Amur is Adad." Addu, as is well known, is also the god of the mountains. $MAR\text{-}TU = Amurru = bêl\ shadî$, *i.e.*, "lord of the mountain." $KUR\text{-}GAL$ ($= Amurru$) $= shadû\ rabû$, *i.e.*, "the great mountain."

---

[1] *Z. A.*, VI, 303 ff.
[2] *Rel. Bab. und Ass.*, p. 222.
[3] *K. A. T.³*, p. 433.
[4] Cf. Jensen, *K. B.*, VI, p. 563.
[5] Cf. III *R.*, 67, Rev. *c–d*, 51.

In this connection we are reminded of the epithets Shaddai, Elyon and Ṣur (שדי, עליון and צור) of the Old Testament, as well as the conception the Syrians had of the nature of Israel's God when they said, "Yahweh is a god of the hills," 1 Kings 21 : 28.[1]

As has been shown, there are other designations of this deity, namely, *Mur, Mer, Bur, Bir*, etc.[2] These seem to be variations of the name *Mar*.[3] And that being true, *Bir-Hadad* would mean "Mar is Hadad," which later may have been misunderstood by the Hebrews who, perhaps influenced by the Assyrian *Mar* (see p. 162), considered it to be the Aramaic *bar*, "son." Moreover, I simply desire to emphasize in this connection that this deity is indigenous in the West, and was introduced from that land into Babylonia.

NUSKU.

Nusku is also recognized as an original solar deity. The names of the *Ḥarran Census*[4] show that this deity was prominently worshiped in Haran under the name of *Naskhu*, where there was a temple devoted to him. Some hold that the deity was imported from Nippur, but exactly the reverse is more likely to be the

---

[1] See Ward, "The Origin of the Worship of Yahwe," *Amer. Jour. Sem. Lang.*, April, 1909, p. 175 ff. Also see Part I, p. 88.

[2] See Jastrow, *Rel. Bab. und Ass.*, p. 146; also Hommel, *Aufsätze*, p. 220, and Zimmern, *K. A. T.*[3], p. 445 ff.

[3] Hilprecht, *Assyriaca*, p. 77, note 1, says *Me-ir* (= *Mir*) is identical with *Bir* or *Mur*.

[4] See Johns, *Assyrian Doomsday Book*, p. 12.

case, namely, that *Nusku* was originally a Western deity, and that *Naskhu* represents the more ancient writing of the name.

ISHUM.

Ishum, the messenger of Nergal, is also a fire- or pest-god. This deity appears as the faithful attendant of *Urra*, who is the same as Nergal, and is in all probability the same as the West Semitic *Esh* (אש) discussed above.

ṢARPANITUM.

Ṣarpânitum, the consort of Marduk, is also a solar deity, and means "brightness" or "shining."[1] There can be no question but that the name is Semitic, and is a formation in *ân* from צרף. The figures of this deity on the seal cylinders, Doctor Ward thinks, are borrowed from the Syro-Hittite representations of the chief goddess of the West (see below).

BU-NE-NE.

Another variation of this solar deity is the charioteer or companion of Shamash, worshiped especially at Sippar, whose name is *BU*(or *SIR*)-*NE-NE*. *SIR* = *nûru*, and *NE-NE* can equal *ishâti* (plural), and the name can mean "Light of the great fire." In the late period *MUR* is used interchangeably with *SIR-NE-NE*.[2]

---

[1] Cf. Zimmern, *K. A. T.*³, p. 375.
[2] Cf. Tallqvist, *Z. A.*, VII, p. 279.

This sign is usually read *ḤAR*, but *MUR* might be preferable. An interesting variant of the name *ᵈMUR-ibni, Dar.* 395 : 20, is to be found in *Dar.* 396 : 18, where the same name is written *ᵈUTU-ibni*. It is not improbable that *UTU* is to be read *Bir*, which is a variant of *Mer, Mur*, etc.[1] This explanation, if correct, would throw interesting light on the name of the hero of the Babylonian deluge story, *UTU-napishtim*, which name may also be read *Bir-napishtim* (see Part I). The associations of the god *MUR*, considered in connection with the possible variant readings, show that it is a solar deity.

MALIK.

And who will question that *Malik* is West Semitic or Arabic instead of Babylonian, perhaps originally only an epithet,[2] but later considered to be a name? This well known deity is prominently associated with Shamash and *SIR-NE-NE* at Sippar. This fact is interesting when considered in connection with the familiar name *Uru-milki* and *Milki-Uru,* found early and late in Babylonia, as well as among the Western Semites. In the Manishtusu Obelisk the name *Malik-ZI-IN-SU* occurs. The name of Sargon's scribe is *Shum-Malik*.[3] These occurrences show that the

---

[1] See above and *K. A. T.*³, p. 443 ff.
[2] See Moore's article, "Molech," *Enc. Bib.*, also Barton in *Jewish Encyclopædia*; and Zimmern, *K. A. T.*³, p. 469.
[3] *Vor. Bib.*, I, 164g.

name was introduced into Babylonia in the early Semitic period.

A study of the early history of these recognized Semitic Babylonian solar deities leads us to certain important conclusions. In the first place, we are impressed with the fact that nearly all the important Semitic Babylonian gods are sun-deities, and that they are not indigenous to the land. The earliest traces of the more important are synchronous with the earliest references to the Semites in Babylonia. And after we realize that there must be assumed a great antiquity for the Amorites and their culture, and finding that they, including the Aramæans, had the same deities as the Semitic Babylonians, we can postulate, after a consideration of all that is known, that the Semitic Babylonians were originally Western Semites; and especially as the elements in question, generally speaking, do not belong, as far as we know, to other early peoples.

Dr. William H. Ward, the eminent authority on Babylonian seals, informs me that the sun-god is one of the most favorite themes of the Babylonian and Syrian seal cylinders. For years he has made a study of Babylonian and Syro-Hittite seals. His comparison of the forms of Babylonian gods with the forms of the Syro-Hittite deities as depicted in their art has led him to the conviction that the forms originated in the West. That is, from the art of that region were derived the representations of Marduk and Amurru (*MAR-TU*) at different times from the more dignified god who appears in the Syro-Hittite art usually without weapons. Marduk is represented simply holding his scimitar downward, while Amurru the same god is represented with one hand to his breast, holding a short rod.

Ṣarpânitu, the naked goddess on seals, who is the consort of Marduk, corresponds to the naked goddess on the Syro-Hittite seals, very likely the wife of Tarkhu, the chief god of the Hittites. The fourth Babylonian god in the art of the Semitic Babylonians coming from the West is Adad, who holds a thunderbolt and weapon over his head, and leads a bull (for the thunder). In the Hittite art this god, usually called Teshub, bears other weapons such as the club, axe, etc. The earlier art of the Tigro-Euphrates valley back of the time of Gudea, in the opinion of Dr. Ward, does not show traces of this influence (see also page 87).

We have only to recall how very frequently the name of *Amurru* ($^d MAR$-TU) occurs on the seal cylinders of the Semitic Babylonians as the patron god of the individual, and especially in contrast with the official use of the names of the gods in the inscriptions. This is reasonably explained according to the theory proposed in these discussions, namely, that the great deity known to the Amorites as *Amurru*, perhaps also *Ûru*, when brought into Babylonia received in different localities different names. That is, in these various centers, which were really independent principalities with their own guilds or schools of scribes, the Semites having probably already an alphabetic script, and speaking a foreign tongue, were totally dependent at first, and perhaps for centuries, upon the Sumerian scribes of the land for everything that was written in cuneiform upon clay or stone. This involved on the part of the Sumerian scribes a determination of the form in which their personal names and deities should appear; and as a result these forms in time became conventionalized, just as hundreds of other words in their vocabulary which are Sumerian.

In writing the name of the solar god of the Semites, the Sumerian scribes at Sippar used the character which represented their own sun deity. The old original Semitic name Shamash prevailed, perhaps by reason of the fact that Sippar was in the early period a powerful Semitic center. This, of course, is very evident in comparison with Nippur, where the contracts in the First dynasty are still written in Sumerian, as is shown by the texts recently published by Poebel (*B. E.*, Vol. VI, part 2). At Babylon, the scribes did the same thing and used in writing the name of this imported sun-god their own *UTU* or *UTUG*, prefixing *AMAR* to distinguish this Western god from their own god. At Cutha, there seem to have been several different forms of the name of the deity, namely, *Urru*, "The light"; *NE-URU-GAL*, "Light of the great *Ûru*"; *LUGAL-URU*, "King or Lord *Ûru*"; *U-ri-gal*, etc. Elsewhere the deity was written *IB* or *Urash*, *i.e.*, "The *Amar-Esh*"(?), and *NIN-IB*, his consort, which later was masculinized and considered to be *EN-Martu*, "the Ba'al Amurru," or *EN-Mashtu*, "The lord *Mashtu*."

Naturally the attributes of this sun-god, although originally the same deity, would develop differently, due to different conditions or influences. In the later centuries, the petty principalities were brought together into political unions, and there was a grouping of the deities into a pantheon, when their original solar significance was more or less lost sight of, with the exceptions of Shamash at Sippar. If this conclusion is not accepted, then it must be assumed either that the entering Semites adopted the Sumerian *UTU* sun-cult of Larsa in Southern Babylonia, and modified it in accordance with their own ideas by giving it different names, or it must be assumed that they came from different quarters, in each one of which a solar god was worshiped under a different name. That is, if the theory advanced is not correct, the Semites living in Sippar came from one district, while the devotees of Marduk and those that worshiped other sun-deities came from other localities. Such conclusions naturally would involve us in great difficulties, and would indicate a strange development of sun worship as well as a state of affairs rather difficult to comprehend. In the light of all the facts known, it seems that the only conclusion at which we can arrive is that the Babylonians, generally speaking, were originally Western Semites, and that they brought with them their solar worship from the West.

OTHER GODS:—ASHUR.

The chief deity of the Assyrian pantheon also seems to be an importation from the West. The appearance of the name Ashur in Assyria is found in the earliest inscriptions from that land. The fact that the name does not occur in the early Babylonian inscriptions precludes saying the deity is Babylonian. Further, the fact that the name is written *A-usar*, *A-shir*, *A-shur*, *Ash-shur*, etc., points to a foreign origin.

The deity figures prominently in the Cappadocian tablets, some of which belong to the latter part of the third millennium B.C. It also occurs in the Amarna letters. It is found in the Old Testament אשר אלה. The name is in the Phœnician עבראסר אשרשלח, etc., and in the Aramaic אסרמלך,[1] אשרחב, etc., and perhaps even in the name of the tribe and city *Asher* and *Asshurim*, Gen. 25 : 3, etc.[2]

These occurrences of the name in the inscriptions of the West point to West Semitic origin, and the association of such elements as *Malik* even suggests that it may be solar. When we take into consideration also the fact that other prominent Assyrian deities, such as Shamash, Amur, Adad, Urra, Dagan, etc., are Western; and that the study of the so-called Syro-Hittite art shows that the West has furnished the form of several deities for Assyria, it would seem that the Assyrian culture arose through migrations from the West instead of from Babylonia.[3]

---

[1] Cf. *A-shir-ma-lik* and *A-shur-ma-lik* in the Cappadocian inscriptions.

[2] Hommel, *Die vier Paradiesesflüsse*, p. 278, holds the deity is from the West.

[3] Winckler, *History of Babylonia and Assyria* (Craig's translation, p. 181), holds that the representations of the Assyrian physiognomy is Jewish.

While it is not improbable that the temple of Ashur in the city Ashur was founded by a Hittite ruler, as has been maintained; and that there was a brief Hittite rule over Babylonia,[1] the elements which made up the culture of Assyria are not Hittite but Semitic. If the center from which the Semites came is Amurru, the influence of Hittite art upon the Semitic would be easy to understand, because the dominant power in Amurru at 2000 B.C. was Hittite.

Assyria may have been originally a colony from Babylonia, but for the present this view must be regarded as entirely hypothetical. The early rulers seem to have been foreigners, for example, *Irishum*[2] the son of *Ḫallu*,[3] *Igur-kapkapu*, *Pudi-El*,[4] *Ushpia*,[5] *Kikia*,[6] etc. Later rulers' names are mostly compounded with the West Semitic *Ashur, Adad,* and *Shamshi*.

Considering the date of the Cappadocian tablets and the fact that nearly all, although coming from different localities, contain this element, it must be admitted that the idea that those bearing these names represent Assyrian colonists, when Assyria is scarcely known in the inscriptions of the East, is exceedingly precarious. If *Ashera* is the consort of this deity, the fact that the

---

[1] See Ungnad, *B. A.*, VI, 5, p. 13, and Jastrow, "Hittites in Babylonia," *Revue Semitique*.

[2] Cf. *I-ri-si-im*, in the Cappadocian tablets.

[3] Cf. *Ḫalili, Ḫalia*, etc., in *B.E.*, XV; perhaps to be associated with *Ḫaligalbat*.

[4] Cf. the biblical Pedahel and Pedaiah.

[5] Cf. the Cassite *Ush-bi-Saḫ, B.E.*, XV.

[6] Cf. *Kikia, B.E.*, XIV, and Ungnad, *B.A.*, VI, 5, p. 13.

name was common in the West, and not in the East, is strikingly significant. In this she has her parallel in *Antum*, also apparently a Western goddess.

ISHTAR.

Not only do we have the West Semitic Asher in Babylonia, but *Ashera* the chief goddess. A great diversity of opinion seems to exist with reference to the origin of the name and cult of *Ishtar*. Haupt holds that the deity came from the name *Ashur*.[1] Hommel sees in the *Ashera* of the West the origin of the name.[2] Tiele[3] and Muss-Arnolt[4] see in the name the root *ashâru*, "to be gracious, bless." Barton[5] holds the original habitat of the deity is Arabia, where she was called 'Athtara, and that she entered Babylonia from the South;[6] while Sayce[7] thinks the deity belongs to the non-Semitic Babylonians, *i.e.*, the Sumerians. All that the writer desires to say is that the name of the deity is unquestionably foreign, and that she is the same as

---

[1] Cf. *Jour. Amer. Orien. Soc.*, XXVIII, p. 116. But the change of א to י has not been satisfactorily explained.

[2] *Aufsätze und Abhandlungen*, II, p. 209.

[3] *Bab. und Ass. Geschichte*, p. 533.

[4] *Ass. Dictionary*, p. 118.

[5] Semitic Origins, p. 103 f.

[6] Barton thinks that originally the goddess was brought into the land from Arabia. His chief argument is that with the exception of the Moabite Stone, where it is masculine, and עתר among the Aramæans (see Cooke, *Glossary of Aram. Inscr.*, p. 95 f.), it has the feminine ending in the West, whereas Ishtar of the Babylonians and 'Athtara of the Arabs do not.

[7] *Archæology of the Cuneiform Inscriptions*, p. 338.

142 AMURRU HOME OF NORTHERN SEMITES

Ashratu,[1] the *bêlit ṣeri*, as represented by the Assyrians, the Astarte of the West, and consort of Amurru;[2] and that it seems highly probable that the biblical *Ashera* is the same, which appears to be the feminine of *Ashur*.

At Erech, the same prostitution that attended the worship of Ashtoreth in Canaan existed in the cult of Ishtar. At Bismaya, also dedicated to Ishtar, Dr. Banks informs me he found jars containing the bodies of small infants, as were found in the high places of Canaan, and indications of the same lewd practices of the Erech cult.[3] The question arises, were these rites introduced into Canaan from Babylonia, or *vice versa*? Another alternative, of course, is that there was a common source; but of this we have no knowledge. As has been said, Erech was essentially a Semitic city. The very fact that this phase of the cult did not exist generally in Babylonia and Assyria, where Ishtar was worshiped, although Herodotus speaks of it at Babylon, would speak against its origin being fixed in Babylonia; and especially as it was so thoroughly rooted in the West.

ANU AND ANTUM.

ANNA, the patron deity of Erech, is generally recognized as a deity of the Sumerians. Although the cults

---

[1] Cf. עשתרת, Gen. 14 : 5, also *K. B.*, V, 142 : 10 and 237 : 21. The use of ע is to be noted, for if it is the same name the change ע to א or א to ע has taken place.

[2] See Jensen, *Zeit. für Ass.*, XI, p. 302.

[3] The usual explanation is that the bodies represent the offering of the first-born. Another suggestion may be that perhaps they are the offspring resulting from these debased rites.

of *Anu* and *Ishtar* of Erech are clothed in a Semitic garb, and the town is "essentially a Semitic city," I do not wish even to suggest that *ANNA* might be Semitic.

There are some reasons, however, for venturing the suggestion that a Semitic deity *Anu* was introduced into Babylonia from the West, some of whose characteristics were associated with the cult of the so-called Sumerian *ANNA*.

Anu figures prominently in the early Assyrian inscriptions with other West Semitic deities, as *Ashur, Shamash, Adad, Ishtar*, etc. Perhaps the only name of the early period compounded with *Anu* (see Langdon, Index to *V. B.*, I) is *Anu-banini*, king of Lulubi. In this ruler's inscription, *Anu* is the first deity mentioned. Thureau-Dangin (*V. B.*, I, p. 173) regards this inscription probably earlier than the Ur dynasty. *Anu* figures also in the names *Gimil-Anim, Pî-sha-Ana* and *Idsha-Ana* of the Cappadocian tablets. It is perhaps also in the deity's name *Anammelek* (2 Kings 17 : 31).

Especially significant is the fact that the consort *Antum* is not recognized in Babylonia. It occurs in the Assyrian inscription of Agumkakrime, and in the late name *A-na-at-da-la-ti* (Johns, *A. D. D.*, p. 317). It occurs in the early inscription of *Anu-banini*, king of Lulubi, found at Seripul. It occurs in the old Canaanite names of towns '*Anathoth* and *Bêth-'Anath*; and perhaps is in the name '*Anath*, father of Shamgar. Prof. Montgomery calls my attention also to the name of the Amori tehero '*Aner* (Genesis 14 : 13), for which the Samaritain Hebrew gives the variant *An-ram*, perhaps intended for *Anu-ram*. It is usually understood to have been carried to Egypt as early as the 18th dynasty (*Asien*, p. 313). In short, the absence of the consort in Babylonian literature and its occurrence in the West must be indicative of its origin.

NABU.

Nabû, another important Babylonian deity, who does not make his appearance very early, at least in this Semitic form, also seems to be of West Semitic origin. The deity is prominently mentioned in the West Semitic inscriptions as an element in names.[1] The mountain which was the place of Moses' death was dedicated to this god. Like Addu, Amurru, Dagan and other West Semitic names, Nabû is frequently found in the cuneiform inscriptions of the Neo-Babylonian period in distinctively West Semitic names, as *Nabû-idri'*, *Nabû-rapa'*, etc., etc.[2] And also when the fact is considered that Marduk, Nergal, Nanâ, Gula, and other deities bearing names distinctively Babylonian are not found in the West Semitic nomenclature, we are led to feel that Nabû must be an importation from the West. Because of the deity's relation with fertility, Jensen[3] regarded Nabû as originally a solar deity. His association or identification with Nusku would support this view. However, the evidence on this is too scant to arrive at any conclusion.

---

[1] See Lidzbarski, *Nord. Sem. Epig.*, p. 20 ff.
[2] See Tallqvist, *Namenbuch*, and *B. E.*, Vols. IX and X.
[3] *Kosmologie*, p. 239.

AMURRU IN CUNEIFORM INSCRIPTIONS 145

SIN.

The moon-god *Sin* seems to be West Semitic. Nannar, at Ur (*Urumma*), being also a moon-god, later became identified with Sin by the Semites, but the chief habitat of the latter, as far as is known, seems to be Haran. The large number of personal names compounded with *Sin*, or rather *Si-'*, found in the *Ḫarran Census*[1] shows how popular the cult was in that city. Although the Assyrian scribes did not use the determinative in connection with this deity in the *Ḫarran Census*, and instead of one of the usual ideograms for *Sin* wrote the name *Si-'* (occasionally *Si* and *Se*, yet compare the variant *Si* for $^d Sin$ in Ungnad, *V. S.*, III: 18), we conclude that the breathing represented a pronunciation peculiar to the district.

The name was written *Sin* outside of Haran in Babylonia, Palestine, and Arabia; cf. also the "Wilderness of Sin" and "Mt. Sinai." Notwithstanding this fact the deity may be Aramæan. In an Aramaic inscription published by Pognon[2] the name of the god is written *Si* (סי) as well as *Su* (סו). It is in the name ברכסו, which Pognon reads *Bar-iksu*.[3] Without any doubt *Si* (סי) is here the moon-god *Sin*, written practically the same as in the tablets belonging to the place of his principal habitat. Perhaps also we may see the same element in the name Sisera and Sihon (סיסרא and סיחון).

---

[1] See Johns, *Ass. Doomsday Book*, p. 13.

[2] *Inscriptions Sémitiques*, p. 114.

[3] Grimme, *O. L. Z.*, 1909, p. 17, considers the deity to be "*Si* = Siebengottheit."

10

146 AMURRU HOME OF NORTHERN SEMITES

If the conjecture that the original form of the deity is *Si'*, *Se*, or *Su*,[1] should prove to be correct, is it not possible to see in *EN-ZU*, the ideogram for Sin, the Sumerian element *EN*, Lord, and the Semitic *Su* or *Si*, a formation like *EN-Mashtu*; and on the principle that *Nin-su-gir* appears *Nin-gir-su*, *EN-Su* might be written *Su-EN* or *Si-EN* = Sin. Compare the name *En-na-Zu-in* found in a Cappadocian tablet.[2] If the deity is of West Semitic origin this will account for the Babylonian form. This, let me add, is only offered as a plausible conjecture, for the *n* of *Sin* in Babylonian and the other West Semitic dialects may represent what the scribes in the Haran district intended by the breathing in *Si'*.

DAGAN.

It is quite evident that *Dagan* is also a West Semitic deity[3] who was early introduced into Babylonia. The name of the deity, with the determinative for god, is found on the Obelisk of Manishtusu. In the 37th year of Dungi a temple is dedicated to Dagan. In the dynasty of Isin, probably West Semitic, *Ishme-Dagan*, one of the rulers, doubtless bears a West Semitic name. *Dagan*, as is well known, was the god of Gaza and Ashdod. The place name *Bêth-Dagan*, and the name of the Canaanite, *Dagan-takala*, who is one of the writers

---

[1] The form of the deity *Zû*, which is also written *Zî* and *Zâ* in the Legion *Zû*, is at least to be noted here.

[2] Identified as Sin by Hommel.

[3] Cf. Clay, *Jour. Amer. Orien. Soc.*, XXVIII, and Meyer, *Geschichte des Altertums*, p. 468.

of the Amarna letters, point to Palestine or Amurru as the original habitat of this deity. Compare also *I-ti-Da-gan* in the Cappadocian tablets, published by Sayce in a recent number of the *Babyloniaca*. The West Semitic names found in the tablet from Ḫana (see Ungnad, *B. A.*, VI, 5, p. 28) also support this view. In these tablets the deities *Shamash* and *Dagan* are found in the oath formula. The tablets said to have been found at Ed-Deir support the views of those who have held that his worship radiated from the highlands between Palestine and Mesopotamia.

LAḪMU AND LAḪAMU.

The god *Laḫmu* and goddess *Laḫamu*, which occur in the Marduk-Tiamat legend and in a few syllabaries and incantation texts, also appear to be Amoritish. The fact that they play no part in the pantheon indicates foreign origin. As has been pointed out by others, *Laḫmu* probably is one of the elements in *Bêth-Leḫem*, which was the name of two cities in Palestine.

Other distinctively Semitic gods may be regarded in the same way. Several of those discussed above under the heading "Other Deities," may prove eventually to have been solar in their original habitat; but more evidence must be forthcoming before this can be determined. This much can be said, they are in all probability West Semitic deities.

Besides the argument based on the culture and religion, the Babylonian script offers strong evidence in support of this thesis.

148 AMURRU HOME OF NORTHERN SEMITES

It is a well established fact that the northern group of Semitic languages, *i.e.*, the Amoraic, Aramaic and Assyro-Babylonian, are more closely related to each other than they are to the languages of the southern group, namely, Arabic and Abyssinian. Inasmuch as there are so many elements that the northern cultures have in common, it seems natural to assume that they had a common origin; and the question arises which is the earlier.

The Babylonian script, as is understood, is an adaptation of the Sumerian cuneiform system for the Semitic language that was brought into the country; and in that script the weaker consonants or radicals are elided, or contracted, or appear as vowels. A study of the script of the Northern group makes it most difficult to understand, if the Babylonian is the older language, how the weak radicals, which had disappeared, should have been restored, and the roots correctly introduced in the alphabetic script of the Western languages. For example, it is difficult to understand how *Bêl*, *Ûru* and *Ti'amat*, or the corresponding *bêlu*, *ûru* and *tâmdu*, could be correctly introduced as בעל, אור and תהום. Naturally some Babylonian loan words[1] are found in the West, but would we not expect generally to find many peculiar formations, due to this transportation and transformation. The differences in the verbal formation, and other peculiarities of the Babylonian,

---

[1] More discrimination should hereafter be exercised in declaring words which the Babylonian and Hebrew have in common to be of Babylonian origin.

due to the fact that the written language was created by Sumerian scribes or those familiar with the Sumerian writing (who constructed grammatical rules in order to use their own script for the Semitic tongue that appeared in their midst), would also show themselves prominently in the Western languages, if the influence of Babylonia had been what is claimed for it.

We have seen that in the earliest known period of Semitic Babylonian history, which belongs to the age apparently not far removed from the time when the Semites entered Babylonia, *Amurru* was already an important factor in the affairs of nations, and that it was a land which the great world conquerors of Babylonia, both Sumerian and Semitic, took pains to subjugate. This leads to the conclusion that the culture of *Amurru* was at that period already old. This, as we have seen in Part I, is fully substantiated by the Egyptian inscriptions. We have also seen that in the earliest Semitic period of Babylonian history, the most important deity that we recognize as Semitic belongs to the land *Amurru*, and especially that this sun-deity played a most important part in the Babylonian religion and nomenclature. And we have further seen that there are reasons for asserting that nearly all the Semitic deities of early Babylonian history can be shown to be originally West Semitic, that is either Amoritish or Aramaic.

Taking everything into consideration, and especially the fact that the Semites are not indigenous to Babylonia, it seems reasonable to postulate that they came from the West.

AMURRU IN WEST SEMITIC INSCRIPTIONS

IN the Old Testament, the only form of the name of the land known as *Amurrû*, generally recognized, refers to the inhabitants, and appears with the Gentilic ending, *i.e.*, 'Amorî (אֱמֹרִי, *LXX* is Ἀμορραῖος); and in nearly every instance the word has the article. The Amorites are considered to be the descendants of the fourth son of Canaan (cf. Gen. 10 : 16 and 1 Chron. 1 : 14). They form part of the ancient inhabitants of Palestine, and yet under the name are included the Canaanites, Girgashites, Hittites, Hivites, Jebusites and Perizites, and once (Gen. 15 : 19–21) the Kenites, Kenizzites, Kadmonites and Rephaim. From the Old Testament it would seem that Amorite history reached far back into antiquity, and that the people had maintained their identity down to the Hebrew period. As a nation, however, they had then begun to disintegrate and were losing prestige. The domination of the Hittites in the middle of the second millennium doubtless brought this about. But there is every indication that they were originally an extensive and powerful people, whose chief location was the mountainous region north of what we now recognize as Palestine, covering the district, it seems, as far north as the Orontes; in other words, to the Hittite land.

In the Old Testament they are generally represented as a people living in the highlands. Palestine in the early period seems to have been extensively controlled by the Amorites. Macalister, in the excavations at Gezer, finds traces of a people he calls Amorites at a date which he fixes about 2500 B.C. Naturally there may be more ancient sites in the land than Gezer where the Amorites lived. After this period the occupation of the city seems to have been supplanted by the Israelites, about the middle of the second millennium. Although the Amorites had their day and ceased to be a factor as a people, they held various cities for centuries succeeding the occupation of Canaan by Israel.[1]

As is well known, four-fifths of the letters found in Egypt at Tel el-Amarna, which represent the official and friendly correspondence in the Babylonian language of Amenophis III and IV in the fifteenth century B.C., consist of reports and communications from vassals of the Egyptian kings in Western Asia. In this great land the names of districts are practically all Semitic, as *Amurru, Naḥrima, Amqi, Ziri-Bashani* and *Gar*. As geographical names frequently are retained from one era to another, we realize that the inhabitants of the land prior to this age in all probability were Semitic. We reach the same conclusion when such names of the

---

[1] For a discussion of the Amorites based upon the Old Testament see W. M. Müller, in the article "Amorites" in the *Jewish Encyclopædia*; Sayce, in Hastings' *Dictionary of the Bible*; or Barton, in the *One Volume Dictionary*, p. 271. Also Barton, *ibid.*, p. 110, on the "Canaanites."

152 AMURRU HOME OF NORTHERN SEMITES

cities are taken into consideration, as *Ṣurri, Ṣiduna, Gubla, Qideshu, Urusalim* and others, some of which at least are considered to have had a great antiquity.

The predominance of Semitic personal names is so evident in these letters that it is only necessary to mention the fact. The consideration of the names Abdi-Ashirta, his son Aziru, and others, indicates their Semitic origin. Further, it is sufficient to recall that the letters from this great region betray the fact that the native tongue of the writer is Hebraic. In other words, these letters make us acquainted with the fact that the culture of this land, which is Semitic, is of a highly developed character, indicating that, back of what we have become familiar with, there must be a long period of development covering millenniums. The names clearly indicate also that the chief deity of this region was solar, who, as we have seen above, appears under different names or epithets, as *Ûru, Adad, Milku, Urash, NIN-IB, Shamash*, etc.

The theory advanced years ago,[1] that the Amorites depicted on the walls of the Egyptian temples and tombs with short and pointed beards, blue eyes and reddish hair, high forehead and rather prominent cheek bones, thin lips and straight noses, show that they physiologically were Indo-Europæans, does not seem to have found acceptance. The monuments show that the Amorites represent in practically every instance a Semitic people (see p. 29). This would imply that in that age

---

[1] Sayce, *Early History of the Hebrews*, p. 42.

already the name may have been used simply from a geographical point of view.

Macalister found, as the result of his two years' diggings at Gezer in Palestine, where he discovered an Amorite high place, that the earliest aborigines were troglodytes.[1] They were small in stature, being on an average an inch or two over five feet in height. A study of the partially cremated skulls and bones by Professor Alexander Macalister, of Cambridge, led to the conclusion that they represented a people of a pre-Semitic occupation of that city. Fortunately the mode of burial by the Semites at a later period was by inhumation. The remains show that they were taller, stronger and a larger boned race than the earlier people. They seem to have made their appearance, according to Stewart Macalister, the explorer, at about 2500 B.C. "These Semites," he thinks, "had relations with Egypt as early as the Twelfth dynasty. They made or began the great megalithic high place; practised sacrifice of the first born and foundation sacrifice; had many varieties of grain for food; made pottery of the so-called early pre-Israelite type; were strongly influenced by Egypt, but much less by Babylonia. The beginning of the late Semitic period synchronizes with the settlement of the Hebrews in Canaan, but these do not seem to have had undisputed possession of Gezer."[2]

The names of Amorites mentioned in the Old Testament do not throw much light upon their origin. While

---
[1] See *Bible Side Lights from the Mounds of Gezer*, p. 43.
[2] Lyon, *Harvard Theological Review*, 1908, p. 82.

some are called Amorites, that term may have been used very early in the sense that it was in later biblical times, when all the peoples were included under that general name (see above), Mamre, Eshcol and Aner (Anram). Og and Sihon[1] are mentioned as Amorites. In Joshua 10 : 3, Hoham[2] of Hebron, Piram of Jarmuth, Japhia of Lachish, and Debir of Eglon are mentioned as Amorite kings. These names, which can be derived from Semitic stems, throw light upon the situation. The name of Adoni-Zedek, the king of Jerusalem, who associated himself with the others, contains well recognized Semitic elements. The same is true of Malki-Zedek, king of Salem (perhaps Jerusalem, see Appendix), of an early period.

It is unfortunate that we do not have more names of persons in the Old Testament who can be identified unmistakably as Amorites. It is certain, however, that a large percentage of Old Testament names of the early period in Palestine are Semitic, the same as the names in the Amarna letters, which represent the inhabitants of Canaan prior to the entrance of Israel. We have, therefore, every indication that not only the language of the land was what is called Hebraic, but the names and religious cult indicate at least that most of the inhabitants were Semitic.

---

[1] סיחון perhaps contains the element סי, *i.e.*, moon-god Sin; see above.

[2] Hoham is found in Minæan, cf. הוחם = *Hauḫam*; cf. Hommel, *Ancient Hebrew Tradition*, p. 221 f. Japhia is perhaps found in the Minæan אליפע = Il-yapi'a; cf. Hommel, *Ancient Hebrew Tradition*, p. 248 f.

The Old Testament supplies us with only scanty ethnological data concerning the Amorites; but if Macalister is correct in his statement that the pre-Israelitish Amorites who occupied Gezer were ethnologically Semitic, we have one very important fact established. Although we know that Aryans or perhaps Turanians were also there, we may conclude that most of the people who lived in that great region, which geographically was called Amurru, from a very early period not only spoke a Semitic language, but in the early period were Semites, and that the land was at a very early time an important center of Semitic culture.

The people from Amurru who appear in the Babylonian tablets generally bear Semitic names. The religion of Amurru that found its way into the Euphrates valley, as we have tried to show, is Semitic. In short, everything points to the fact that the dominant people in the Westland were Semites in the millenniums preceding the Amarna or biblical age. This being true, and bearing in mind that the solar worship of the Babylonian Semites goes back to Amurru, we should find many traces of the worship in that land in which it was indigenous.

Inasmuch as the Amorites figure so prominently in the early period in Palestine, it is reasonable to expect to find in the Old Testament traces of the worship of the chief deity of this people whose name is written *Amurru*,[1]

---

[1] In South Arabian there is a name that seems to be compounded with this element, הלכאמר, king of Saba, cf. Lidzbarski, *Ephemeris*, II, p. 387.

Ûru, etc., as well as אוּר in the Aramaic of Babylonia. In this connection a most interesting passage is to be found in Job 31 : 26, where in parallelism with "moon," אוֹר instead of Shemesh, "sun," is found. The name of the deity seems to be found in אוּרִי, אוּרִיאֵל, אוּרִיהוּ, אוּרִיָּה and שְׂרִיאוֹר. The element *'Ûr* is usually translated "light, flame, or fiery." The Septuagint shows that *'Ûr*, not the common *'Ôr*, "light," is meant. These names, therefore, are to be explained: "My *Ûru*," or simply "*Ûru*" (with a kose suffix); "*Ûru* is God," "*Ûru* is Jahweh," like *Ûri-Marduk* and *Ûru-milki*, see above; and "Shaddai is *Ûru*," cf. צוּרִישַׁדַּי and עַמִּישַׁדַּי, both צוּר and עַמִּי being also equivalents to the names of deities. Before considering other occurrences of the names in the Old Testament, let us inquire whether it occurs in the Amarna letters.

Many of the letters found at Amarna having been written in the fifteenth century B.C., in Amurru, and referring to the land, it is natural to expect to find in them both the name of the country and of the god, *Amurru* or *Ûru*. *Amurru*, as the name of the land, has long ago been recognized, but not the deity. The god, however, is also found in the Amarna letters, in the name *Milkûru*. In these epistles we find a *Milki-ili* and an *Ili-milki*. A parallel formation compounded with *Ûru* would be *Milkûru*, with which *Ûru-milki* of the Sennacherib inscription may be compared. This same name, written *Mil-ki-U-ri*, belongs to a slave in an Assyrian document, dated in the reign of Sargon.[1]

---

[1] Cf. *K. B.*, IV, p. 112.

Perhaps the same name is to be seen in $Uru(MAR-TU)$-Ma-lik in a contract published by Poebel,[1] dated in the First dynasty of Babylon.[2] *Malik* may mean "counsellor," but is the way the name of the deity is written. If so *Uru* in these names seems to represent the deity *Amurru*.

This explanation also throws light on another name, ארמלך, found in a Phœnician inscription at Byblus, belonging to the fourth or fifth century B.C. Lidzbarski[3] translated the first element "light." Cooke[4] compared it with אוריאל and *Urumilki*, and translated "Fire of Milk." The comparison with אור, however, is correct, but the name is the familiar one mentioned above and means "*Uru* is Milk." This defective writing enables us to suggest at least that אראלי, the name of a son of Gad, may be translated "*Uru* is my God." אריאל, usually translated "hearth of El" or "lioness of El," a name applied to Jerusalem, may also contain the element. For a discussion of "The name Jerusalem," which contains *Uru*, see Appendix.

Before the recently published texts of Pognon, *Inscriptions Sémitiques*, reached my hands, Professor Montgomery[5] kindly called my attention to the opening lines of the new Zakir inscription, which reads: "The stele which Zakir of Hamath and La'ash dedicated to

---

[1] *Bab. Exp.*, Vol. VI; pt. 2.
[2] For other formations with *milku*, cf. *K.A T.²*, p. 471.
[3] *Nordsemitische Epigraphik*, 210.
[4] *North Semitic Inscriptions*, p. 20.
[5] See Montgomery, *Biblical World*, February, 1909, p. 158.

El-Ur (אלור)." He suggested for comparison with the deity the name of the antediluvian Babylonian king according to Berosus, namely, 'Αλωρος. Lidzbarski, in a review of the inscription[1] which has since appeared, also admits that the comparison with this name is inviting. Grimme[2] properly regarded ור to be equivalent to *Awar* = Babylonian *Amaru* = *Marduk*.

Unquestionably ור represents the sun-deity *Ûru*. It is a most interesting and important fact that this Aramaic inscription, which belongs to the earliest known in that language, shows that Zakir, king of Hamath and La'ash, dedicated the stele which he erects to El-Ur. The comparison of El-Ur with the first name of the antediluvian Babylonian king 'Αλωρος seems to be most reasonable. But not alone the first of the list, but the second, third, fifth, and perhaps the ninth, contain the name of the deity: 'Αλαπαρος (*Alapaurus, Alaporus*), 'Αμιλλαρος, Μεγαλαρος and perhaps 'Αρδατης. For a fuller discussion of these names see Part I.

The use of El (אל) in connection with the name Ur (ור) is most interesting, especially when we recall El-Shaddai (אל שדי) and El-Elyon (אל עליון) of the Old Testament. Originally, as mentioned above, these may have been epithets, but were not considered as such later on. Prefixing the word for "God" seems to have been a characteristic of the Western Semites. Compare also *Al-Nashḫu-milki, Al-Si'*,[3] *Il-Teḥiri-abi*,

---

[1] *Lit. Zentralblatt*, 1908, p. 582.
[2] *Orient. Lit. Zeit.*, 1909, p. 16.
[3] Johns, *Assyrian Doomsday Book*, p. 15.

AMURRU IN WEST SEMITIC INSCRIPTIONS 159

Il-Teḥri-nûri', and *Bariki-Il-Tammesh*,[1] *Il-Tamesh-dîni*,[2] *Il-Tammesh-ilai*,[3] *Il-Tammesh-natannu*,[4] *Il-Tammesh-nûr*,[5] *Abi-Il-Temesh*,[6] *Il-Teri-ḥanana*,[7] etc. The Rev. Dr. Johns thus regarded the *Al* which is prefixed to the two examples found in his texts. Professor Hilprecht, in his Editorial Preface to my *Babylonian Expedition*, vol. X, p. XIII, asked: "But where did the Assyrians ever pronounce the word for 'god' (אל) in connection with the god's name immediately following in their inscriptions?" He further said: "I do not believe that the people about Ḥarran pronounced it either. *Al* in the name quoted can scarcely be anything else than the article *ăl* or *ĕl*, known from Lidzbarski's list of proper names to have been used in connection with certain deities." Cf. עבר־אלבעלי, גרם־אלבעלי ("The Ba'al"), גמר־אלשהרי ("The moon-god"), etc. Tallqvist[8] accepted Hilprecht's view.

In the first place, the names quoted from Lidzbarski's work to prove the point at issue are not West Semitic nor Aramaic, but are Sinaitic or Arabic. And as a matter of fact it is not known that the article was used in Old Arabic; and further, even if it was, as in the late period, it would not have been used with a

---

[1] Cf. Clay, *B. E.*, X.
[2] Strassmaier, *Nbk.*, 363 : 4.
[3] *Nbn.*, 583 : 18.
[4] *Nbn.*, 497 : 4.
[5] *Cyr.*, 58 : 6.
[6] *Nbn.*, 638 : 4.
[7] *Cyr.*, 177 : 3.
[8] *Neu-babylonisches Namenbuch*, p. 288.

proper name like Shemesh. As stated, the names are Aramæan and the Aramaic did not have an article; so Johns was right in considering this element *Al* to be the word for "god."

These writings ור for the deity's name enable us to explain satisfactorily some West Semitic names. Cooke[1] calls attention to the prefix ור in ורוסן, a name of a priest of Baal-ḥammon in a North Punic inscription from Algiers, and also in ורסכן in a Punic inscription from Thugga, in Eastern Numidia. סכן in the latter doubtless means "prefect" (compare the Assyrian *shaknu*), and is also a divine name or epithet, cf. סכן־יתן. The name could mean "*Ûru* is *Shaknu*," like *Ûru-milk*. יורמנך and ור ידו also contains the element; מנך and ורו both appearing elsewhere as personal names.[3]

If ור in West Semitic inscriptions represents the deity *Ûru*, it is reasonable to expect the name written יר in the Hebrew script, as initial ו usually passes into י. The personal name ירבעל (*LXX*, Ιεροβααλ), according to Judges 6 : 32, is explained "let Baal contend," as if it were a Jussive form. Scholars, appreciating the difficulties involved in this explanation, have proposed that the root is ירה, as in ירו אל and ירי אל (see Brown's *Heb. Dic.*, p. 937). The transliterations of the *LXX*, namely, 'Αρβααλ, 'Ιαρβααλ, 'Ιεαροβααλ, 'Ιεραβααλ, seem to support the proposed change. Yet in all probability the name is to be interpreted "Ur is Baal."

---

[1] *North Semitic Inscriptions*, p. 146.
[2] Lidzbarski, *Nord. Epig.*
[3] Cf. Lidzbarski, *Nord. Epig.*

AMURRU IN WEST SEMITIC INSCRIPTIONS 161

It would be rather surprising if the god *Ûru* or *Amurru* were not found in the tablets discovered in Cappadocia which have been published by Delitzsch,[1] Sayce[2] and Pinches.[3] *Shamash, Ishtar, Ashur, Anu, Adad, Malik, Dagan*, etc., have been recognized, but not, as far as I can see, the god *Amurru*. I venture, however, to suggest that this element is to be recognized in names like *Amur-ilu, A-mur-Ashur, A-mur-Shamash, A-mur-Ishtar*. These naturally might be translated, with Hommel,[4] *Amur-ilu*, "I beheld the god"; but it seems to be reasonable, in the light of these investigations, to propose that the name signifies "*Amur* is god." Compare also *Ili(NI-NI)-a-ma-ra*,[5] Pinches, *ibid.*, p. 50.

Finding that in Babylonia *Mar* was extensively used alongside of *Amar* or *Ûr*, we should expect to find the same to be the case in the Westland itself, and especially because of the frequent change of מ and ו. The deity or epithet occurs in the Aramaic and Phœnician inscriptions, cf. מריחי, מרסמך, מרברך, etc. It has been conjectured that מר, originally used in an appellative sense, meant "lord" (מרא), and

---

[1] *Kappadokische Keilschrifttafeln*, Vol. XIV, A. K. G. W., pp. 207 ff.

[2] *Babyloniaca*.

[3] *Annals of Archæology and Anthropology*, Vol. I, No. 3, p. 49 ff.

[4] *Anc. Heb. Trad.*, p. 67.

[5] This makes it plausible to assume that perhaps such names as *Amur-bêli* and *Amur-Sin* of the First dynasty, cf. Ranke, *P. N.*, p. 66, and also *Ilima-amur*, quoted by Hommel, *Anc. Heb. Trad.*, p. 141, n., may also contain the same element. Compare such parallel names as *Ili-ma-a-bi* and *Ili-ma-a-hi*, Ranke, *P. N.*, p. 101, and the Hebrew אבימאל.

11

was afterwards used as a title of a deity. Hoffman[1] translates מריח "Adonis lebt." This is not impossible, but a better explanation would be to take מר (*Mar*) as another form of ור (*War*), etc.—in other words, the element under discussion. Through the kindness of Professor Montgomery my attention has been called to the name of a god or demon, *i.e.*, a depotentized deity, written מראלהא in Pognon, *Inscriptions Sémitiques* (p. 82). The same demon occurs in a Syriac incantation bowl published by Stübe.[2] In the light of the above facts, it seems reasonable to identify this god or demon with the once important deity or epithet of the ancient Amorites, whose cult had practically disappeared, as far as we know, at the time this inscription was written. This may account for the writing *A* and *TUR-USH* for the first element of Bir-Hadad; that is, the signs which had the value *mar* were used (see p. 132).

This form of the name seems to be found also in the name of the land and mountain מריה of Genesis 22 : 2 and 2 Chronicles 3 : 1. Siegfried and Stade regarded the name as a "Wortspiel mit ראה."[3] Concerning the reading of the Peshitta which makes it אמוריא (*i.e.*, "of the Amorites"), Driver thinks "it has some claim to be considered the original one." The Septuagint transliterates the name of the mount upon which Solomon built the temple, 2 Chronicles 3 : 1,

---

[1] *Z. A.*, XI, p. 240.
[2] *Jüdische-Babylonische Zaubertexte*, p. 22.
[3] For other explanations of the name, see Driver in Hastings' *Dictionary of the Bible*, p. 434.

Τοῦ Ἀμορεια. When we consider the meaning of the name Jerusalem (see Appendix), and the passage in Ezekiel 16 : 3 concerning the city, namely, "thy father was an Amorite and thy mother a Hittite," it seems reasonable to suppose that the name Amurru is contained in it, and that the reading preserved by the Septuagint has the fuller form, and also that the place whither Abraham went to sacrifice Isaac, which bears the same name, was in all probability the Amorite land, or rather Amoria proper, which was north of Canaan; for after he had journeyed from Southern Canaan three days, he saw afar off the land Moriah.

The etymology of ancient geographical names offers many difficulties, due to the fact that they may be of great antiquity, or belong to an era of which we have little or no literature. The names may even belong to a people whose existence is shrouded in obscurity, and although they are continued in use, their traditional pronunciation may have suffered so much that they are of comparatively little value in determining the original signification. A great many names of Palestine are known to be of Pre-Israelitish origin. This we learn not only from the Old Testament but from the Amarna tablets, as well as from the lists of such Egyptian kings as Thothmes III., and these (see p. 151) are generally Semitic.

Another personal name, the etymology of which is regarded as obscure, is מריבבעל. It occurs twice in 1 Chronicles 8 : 34, and once in 9 : 40, in which verse also the variant מרי־בעל is found. Some (Brown and Buhl) regard the latter name as an error, while others (Siegfried and Stade and Gray) consider the fuller form an error for מרי בעל. The transliteration of the Septuagint, which is Μεριβααλ, supports the latter view. Brown translates "Baal is advocate"(?). Gray[1] translates "Hero of Baal." The latter is reasonable, but it seems to me, in the light of the above, that the name more probably means "*Mar* is Baal."

---

[1] *Hebrew Proper Names*, p. 201, note 3.

APPENDIX

I. UR OF THE CHALDEES

FOR more than two thousand years efforts have been made to identify the site of "Ur of the Chaldees," the home of Abraham. In recent centuries Urfa or Orfa, which the Greeks called Edessa, had been regarded as the ancient city.[1] Sir Henry Rawlinson in 1855 found bricks at Muqayyar in Southern Babylonia, from which he gathered that the ancient name of the city was *Hur*. Subsequently it was found that the reading of the name was *Urumma*, and in late Babylonian *Urû*, *i.e.*, with a final vowel. The almost general acceptance of this identification is due to the fact that no attractive reasons have been given for any other site. Dillman and Kittel have strongly opposed this identification,[2] but ever since Rawlinson has advanced his view the number of those who have accepted it has steadily increased, so that now it has become quite general. Without attempting an exhaustive treatment of the subject, let us briefly review the facts upon which it rests.

The Old Testament says Terah took Abram and Sarai his wife, Lot his grandson, and brought them forth from Ur of the Chaldees to go into the land of Canaan;

---

[1] For a discussion, as well as references to the literature on the subject, see Pinches, in Hastings' *Bible Dictionary*, IV, p. 835, and Cheyne, in *Encyclopædia Biblica*, IV.

[2] Dillman, *Genesis*, Ed. 6, p. 213 f., and Kittel, *Geschichte der Hebräer*, § 17.

168 AMURRU HOME OF NORTHERN SEMITES

and they came unto Haran and dwelt there. After the death of Terah, the Lord said unto Abraham, "Get thee out of thy country, and from thy kingdom, and from thy father's house, unto a land that I will show thee."

St. Stephen (see Acts 7 : 2, 4) speaks of the place as being in Mesopotamia. While this is rather indefinite, and doubtless an admission that the exact site was not known, it does not point to Shumer, or Southern Babylonia, as the country.

Eupolemus, who lived about 150 B.C., as quoted by Eusebius, speaks of the place of Abraham, who was the inventor of astrology and Chaldean magic, as a city of Babylonia called Καμαρινη, which is called by some the city of Ουριη. As Eupolemus was discussing Hebrew history, it would seem that he reflects the opinion of the Jews at that time.

The mention of Camarina offered a reason for the identification with Muqayyar, the *Urumma* of the early inscriptions, or the *Urû* of the later period, because of the Arabic word *qamar*, meaning "moon," and because Muqayyar in ancient days was dedicated to a moon deity; but especially because Terah, Abraham's father, whom we learn from tradition was an idolater, journeyed to Haran, another city dedicated to the moon-god, where he remained until his death. It is further conjectured that in this late period the ancient name was going out of use, because of the way Eupolemus speaks of the city.

The Talmud, however, as well as some later Arabian

writers, regarded Warka, the Ὀρεχ of the Septuagint, as the city; but this is impossible, as Warka is Erech of Genesis 10 : 10. The very fact that the late Babylonian Jews did not regard *Urumma* as the city, although living in the land, ought to be evidence sufficient to show that the identification of the biblical Ur with that city must have been regarded unfavorably by them.

In the first place, *Urumma*, the name of the city later called *Urû*, was the seat of *Nannar* worship, and not of Sin; the one deity until recently considered Sumerian and the other Semitic, or more precisely Aramaic.[1] *ᵈSHESH-KI* is rendered *Nannar* (IV R., 9, 3a–17a), and also *Sin* (IV R., 1 : 29b; 5, 59a), but these equivalents belong to the late period, when the Sumerian gods were generally identified with the Semitic. In the early period we have no proof of the worship of Sin at *Urumma*. The mere fact that in the late period they were identified one with the other is, therefore, no proof that in pre-Abrahamic days the cults had very much in common, beyond the fact that both represented the worship of moon-gods. And that being true, we might just as well use the argument that Abram came from Babylon, Sippar, Cutha, etc., because the chief deity of these places was a solar deity, and at Haran the fire-god Nusku was also prominently worshiped. The Talmud tells us that Terah worshiped no less than twelve deities, which is quite reasonable, and which makes us feel, knowing a little about those early religions, that

---

[1] In *Semitic Origins*, p. 199 ff., Barton already assumed that there is a Semitic element in Nannar.

the argument has little in it. To identify *Camarina* with *Urumma* because *qamar* in Arabic means "moon" is certainly precarious.

Another difficulty lies in the designation "Ur of the Chaldeans." The geographical term Chaldea or *Kaldu*, written by the Greeks Χαλδαῖοι, although the origin of the name is not understood, does not seem, especially in the early period, to include Lower Babylonia. The word is probably preserved, apart from *Ur-Kasdim*, in *Arfa-Kesed* (*Arphaxad*, perhaps *Urfa*), and in *Kesed*, one of the tribes descending from Nahor (Gen. 22 : 22). However, the traditions, as preserved by Berosus, connect the Babylonians with the Chaldeans.

The argument advanced in favor of *Urumma* as the site of Ur, because of the Chaldean district south of the city, has little or nothing in its favor. That region was known as *Bît-Yakîn*, being inhabited by Chaldeans only some time after 800 B.C. *Yakîn*, which name implies that it is West Semitic, was probably borne by a man who was known as a Chaldean. His estate, *i.e.*, *Bît-Yakîn*, developed into a community of sufficient importance to cause Assyria considerable difficulty in retaining Babylonia, with which it was allied, in endeavoring to regain independence.

The name Abram, as already mentioned in Part I, has at last been found in the cuneiform literature belonging to the patriarch's age. In the tablets from Tell Deilam (*i.e.*, Dilbat), about twenty miles south of Babylon, which are now in the Berlin Museum, the name is written *Aba-rama*, *Abam-ram* and *Abam-rama*.[1]

---
[1] See Ungnad, *Bei. zur Ass.*, VI, 5, p. 60.

UR OF THE CHALDEES

But it does not follow necessarily that the man who bore the name was a Babylonian because he was the son of Awil-Ishtar, a man bearing a Babylonian name. In the same texts there are many examples of men bearing West Semitic names who gave their children Babylonian names; and the reverse is also found in these as well as in the texts of the other periods. This resulted from mixed marriages.[1] The texts show that many Western Semites lived in Dilbat at this time. But what is more important than all else in showing that the name is West Semitic, is the fact that the element *ram* has not been found to exist in the thousands of known Babylonian names, whereas it is a common West Semitic element.

The first element of the name *Abram* is found in all the Semitic dialects, but the second element is Western Semitic. In the Hebrew, besides Abram, and אדנירם, רמיה, מלכירם, אחירם, אבירם, and יהורם occur. In the Phœnician inscriptions compare מלכרם, רמבעל and בעלרם. See also the name in the Murashû texts, *Addu-rammu* (B. E., Vol. X). This element *ram* may be translated "high," or like *Elyon* may have been an epithet of a deity. Moreover, all the ancient traditions show that *Abram* was an Aramæan. The genealogical list of his ancestors in Genesis XI shows that they were Aramæans, certainly not Babylonians. The names of his immediate family are Aramæan. Nahor, the name of his brother, is found in the place

---

[1] See Clay, *Light on the Old Testament from Babel*, p. 403.

name *Til Naḥiri* of the *Ḥarran* census. Compare also Johns, *Deeds and Documents*, 420 : 3; 421 : 5; and the personal names *Naḥarâu* and *Naḥirî*. Milkah, as above, should be connected with the epithet *Malik*. Jiscah in form is also West Semitic. When Abram was commanded to leave Haran, he is told to go out of his country and from his kindred. When Eliezer was sent for Isaac's wife, he was told to go to Abraham's country and to his kindred, in the city of Nahor. When Jacob fled from his brother he went to the ancestral home, and there obtained his wife. The names Bethuel and Laban are West Semitic. In later years their descendants were called Aramæans (compare Genesis 25 : 20, etc.). In short, every bit of evidence that can be brought to bear upon the subject points to the fact that Abraham was not a Babylonian by descent, but that his ancestral home was in Aram. If Ur is located in Babylonia, it then can reasonably be asked why he should have lived in that land.

But, notwithstanding all that has been said with reference to the identification of Ur, scholars as well as the ancients seem to think that Terah and Abram went to Haran from a city some distance away, and that Chaldæa in this connection very probably means Babylonia.[1] The Babylonian Jews, as well as others of ancient times, sought for the city in that land.

In identifying a city, as Ur, there are a number of conditions which should be satisfactorily met. First,

---

[1] Kittel argues that *Kasdim* = *Kaldim* is the land *Kaldia* in Armenia.

UR OF THE CHALDEES 173

the city should be in Chaldæa, preferably not in Shumer, but in Babylonia. Secondly, it should be explained why its location was lost sight of in the late pre-Christian centuries. Thirdly, it ought to be shown why an Aramæan or Western Semite should have come from that city. And fourthly, its name should be '*Ûr* (אוּר).

For some time it has been known that there was a town in the vicinity of Sippar called *Amurru*, which is also written with the usual ideogram *MAR-TU*.[1] This can properly be included in Lower Mesopotamia or Chaldæa.

This city, as far as the writer knows, while apparently a city of some prominence in the time of the First dynasty of Babylon, is not mentioned in the subsequent periods.

As is known, a large proportion of the tablets belonging to this period that have been thus far published come from Sippara and its vicinity. In these tablets it has been found that many of the names of the contracting parties, witnesses in the contracts, officials, and devotees in the Temple documents are West Semitic. Ranke, in his *Personal Names of the Ḫammurabi Dynasty*, p. 33, shows that these people were called "Children of the West Land." His lists of names, as well as those of Poebel,[2] which came from this district, namely, Sippar, show that a large percentage of the residents bore West Semitic names. Toffteen[3] and others have

---

[1] Cf. Meissner, *Altbab. Priv.*, Nos. 42 and 72; also Ranke, *Babylonian Expedition*, Vol. VI, Part I, 42a : 1.

[2] *Babylonian Expedition*, Vol. VI, part 2.

[3] See *Babyl. and Ass. Geog.*, p. 30.

even asserted that the Amorites of the West came from this district (see above). Concerning the way these Western Semites came to live in this locality, we can only theorize. But knowing the later custom of deporting people, and knowing also the account of Chedorlaomer's campaign, how he carried away Lot and the people of Sodom and Gomorrah, we might suggest that they or their ancestors had been carried into exile by some previous Elamite or Babylonian conqueror.

A parallel to this case can be found in the *Business Documents of the Murashû Sons of Nippur*. In them, towns called Ashkelon, Gaza, Heshbon, Bit-Tabalai are located in the vicinity of Nippur in the fifth century B.C. In other words, West Semitic names are introduced for the towns occupied by the Jews in captivity. In these tablets also a great many Jewish names have been found, the descendants of the people whom Nebuchadrezzar placed there in exile. The name of the city Barsip above Carchemish of Gudea's time doubtless is the origin of the Babylonian Borsippa.

And finally, having shown that the West Semitic name $MAR-TU = Amurru = $ אור or 'Ur, and that this is the name of the town in the vicinity of Sippar, we have the only city name Ur of the time of Abraham that is known.

Thus all the requirements that can reasonably be laid down in the identification of the city have been satisfied. The city is in Chaldæa or Babylonia; it thrived at the time that the patriarch lived; its location was later lost sight of; it was inhabited by West Semitic people, and its name is the same as is written in the Old Testament.

II. THE NAME JERUSALEM

THE name Jerusalem has had in the past many different interpretations. As a Hebrew name, formerly it has been considered to mean "The abode of peace," "The possession of peace," "Salem's possession," "A foundation of peace," "Foundation of Shalem," etc. The discovery of the Amarna tablets, which contain the writing *U-ru-sa-lim*, resembling the form *Ursalimmu* of the inscription of Sennacherib, threw new light on the subject. Considered in connection with the Syriac, which is *Urishlem*, scholars realized that Jerusalem, which should have been written in cuneiform something like *Yarûshalim*, was a disguised or perhaps an incorrect writing. This was further corroborated by the writing אורשלם in the Nabatæan inscriptions. The translation "City of Salem," "City of Peace," or "Place of Safety," then became popular, for nearly all scholars seem to have concluded that the elements of the name are a compound of *URU*, which in Sumerian means "city," and the Semitic *shalim*, "peace" or "safety." For example, in his editorial notes to the text of Isaiah,[1] Haupt accepts and fully discusses the name from this point of view: The dialectical form of the Sumerian *URU* is *ERI*, which passed into the Hebrew עיר, "city." The *u*

---

[1] *Polychrome Bible*, p. 100.

vowel after ו in *Urusalim,* he says, is the Sumerian vowel of prolongation. The *i* in the Syriac, Haupt further states, is the vowel of the construct state. *Irushalim,* from which the common form of Jerusalem is derived, represents the dialectic form of *Uru.* The *u* after *r* in *Irushalim* may be due to dissimilation. Pinches, who also accepted the Sumerian origin of the first element, appreciated the difficulty in the genitival relation of the two elements in translating "City of Peace," and suggested the meaning "The city peace," making it a counterpart to or an explanation of the name *Shalem,* "Peace," in Genesis 14.[1]

The theory that the first element is from the Sumerian and means "city" is fraught with difficulties. In the first place, if the theory is correct that the Hebraic or Amoraic עיר is derived from the dialectical form *ERI,* going back to the pure Sumerian *URU,* we must assume that in *Urusalim* we have preserved not the form from which עיר is supposed to have been derived, namely, *ERI,* but the original Sumerian *URU;* or the name would be compounded with pure Sumerian and Semitic elements. Further, inasmuch as we have similar formations as *'Ir Shemesh, 'Ir Naḥash,* etc., belonging to the early period, if the first element of the name *URU* means "city," does it not seem strange that it should have been unrecognized by the ancients that the element had that meaning? Some Sumerian loan words in Hebrew are known, but these are traced back

---

[1] Cf. *The Old Testament in the Light of the Historical Inscriptions,* etc., p. 239 f.

THE NAME OF JERUSALEM 177

to the Sumerian through the Babylonian. If *URU* = *ERI* = '*ir* (עִיר), it must have been borrowed from the Sumerian at an exceedingly remote age by the Amorites, for in the Amarna letters *âlu* is the word used for "city."[1] If the conjecture concerning Mesheq (see p. 125) is correct, it would show that the Babylonian script was used in Damascus, as it was farther north in the third millennium B. C., but a distinction between Babylonian and Sumerian script is to be made. In short, the theory that the first element is Sumerian is exceedingly precarious.

It seems to me that exactly the reverse is the fact, namely, that the dialectical *ERI*, which was by no means in common use in Babylonia, had its origin in the Western Semitic '*ir* (עִיר). Whence is the Babylonian *âlu*, "city"? It surely is not Sumerian, but was introduced into Babylonia when the Western Semites entered the land. They were doubtless tent dwellers (*jôshēb 'ōhel*); and *âlu*, which is from the Arabic *ahl* or Hebrew '*ōhel*, "tent," was naturally an appropriate term for them. *Eri*, which is from the Hebrew עִיר, also came into use in Babylonian.

Two other explanations of this name appear to me to be more reasonable. In the first, the element *Uru* is considered to be the name of the Amorite deity; and in the second, the name of the Amorite land. This seems perfectly reasonable, inasmuch as the Amarna letters show that the name belonged to the age prior to

---

[1] Cf. *K. B.*, V, 45 : 23 and 8 : 30.

the occupation of Israel, when the Amorites were the dominant people of the land.

The name or epithet of the chief deity, as we have seen, of this people was *Ûru*, and a reasonable explanation of "Jerusalem" is that it is compounded with that name and *shalim*, meaning perhaps "*Ûru* is appeased." The second element *shalim* is Semitic, as above stated, being very commonly used in the formation of Babylonian and Assyrian names. It is also found in West Semitic personal names, cf. אשמנשלם, בעלשלם, and נבושלם.[1] Compare also the city *Shalem* of Genesis 14, which may be the same name in an abbreviated form. Compare also the altar name *Yahweh-Shalom* of the Old Testament. For such a theophorous name as *Ûru-shalim*, compare the two altar names *Yahweh-jireh* and *Yahweh-nissi*, also the passage in Jeremiah 36 : 16, where it is said Jerusalem shall be called "Jehovah is our righteousness" (יהוה צדקנו). But especially compare names like *Yabni-el*, *Jezreel*, *Joseph-el*, etc., also the large number of place names of verbal formation; see Glossary in Hommel's *South Arabic Chrestomathy*, under letter *y*.

This gives rise to the question whether the name was originally a place name, or whether it was the name of an individual, which was afterward applied to the estate, manor or town. As an original place name we can compare the names quoted above, and also such Babylonian names as *NIN-IB-ashabshu-iqbi*,[2]

---

[1] See Lidzbarski, *Handbuch*, and Cooke, *North Semitic Inscriptions*.

[2] *B. E.*, Vol. IX, 51 : 5.

Ellil-limmassu,[1] in which case the name *Uru-shalim*, "Ûru is appeased," might have been given to the place on its being rebuilt after an enemy had destroyed it, perhaps when a foundation sacrifice had been offered, as at Jericho.[2] However, if the first element is the name of the deity, *Uru-shalim* appears more likely to be the name of an individual, doubtless an Amorite, "the father of the city," who perhaps was in possession of the hill known as Moriah, or more correctly Amoriah (see above in Part II). As is known, there are many place names among the ancient Semitic as well as other peoples that were once personal names.

The second explanation offered is that the first element is to be regarded as the name of the country, namely, *Amurru* = *Ûru*, in view of such names as Aram-Zobah, Aram-Maachah,[3] etc., and especially if *Shalem* is the original name of the city, which later became the capital of a petty principality, as the Syrian places quoted were. This view finds support in the Amarna letters, for the land or country of the city Jerusalem is several times referred to. That is, like Aram(or Syria)-Maachah, or Aram-Damascus, we would have *Ûru-Shalem*, meaning the Amorite *Shalem*. If these compounds are so common in connection with *Aram*, why should not the same be found to be the case

---

[1] *B. E.*, Vol. XV, for which Meissner suggests the reading *al Bêlnaplissu* (*SHI-MAS-SU*), *Göttingische Gelehrte Anzeigen*, 1908, No. 2, p. 143.

[2] Cf. 1 Kings 16 : 34.

[3] Cf. So. Arabic *Ma'în Miṣrân*, Hommel, *Aufsätze u. Abhandl.*, p. 6.

with *Ûru* or *Amurru*? If this theory is correct, then Shalem of Genesis 14 is very likely to be identified with *Uru-salim*, just as Maachah was known as Aram-Maachah.¹

The writing "Jerusalem" in the Hebrew, which differs so greatly from the Assyrian *Ursalimmu*, is not very difficult to explain. The loss of the initial א, as in אלור, *El-Ûr*, after which the ו being initial passes into י in Hebrew, offers no difficulty. The use of the long vowel following ר must then be regarded as a joining vowel, as in formations like אלוזבד = אליזבד. The Masoretic pointing is like *jᵉqaṭṭel*, which in Arabic is *juqaṭṭilu*, and in Assyrian *uqaṭṭil*.

---

¹ Arpad (ארפד) in Northern Syria was in the early period an Amorite city. The name may be from the root רפד, "to extend," hence ארפד = "terrace," cf. D. H. Müller, *Inschr. Hofmus.*; but it also may mean either *Ûr-Pad*, i.e., the Amorite פד, or "*Ûru* is requited," from פדה, "to redeem, requite," cf. פרהצור, פרהאל, and פריהו. This finds support in the cuneiform inscriptions, where the name is written *ᵃˡᵘArpadda(u)*, but once *ᵃˡᵘMar-pa-da-ai*, Harper, *Letters*, Pt. VII, No. 685, Ov. 19. In the inscription of Gudea, a city *Uru-az*, belonging to this same district, is referred to, cf. Thureau-Dangin, *V. B.*, p. 21. Gudea in an inscription speaks of bringing from *Tidanu*, the mountain of Amurru, marble for *ur-pad-da*, cf. *V. B.* 70, 6 : 17, but the meaning of the passage does not seem to be understood. If the second or third explanation given above should prove correct, there are other geographical names of the Amorite district, the etymology of which is uncertain, that should be considered; for example, *Ur-billum*, etc., of the early period.

III. THE NAME OF SARGON, KING OF AKKAD

THE reading of the name of Sargon, the great ruler of early Babylonian history, has been the subject of considerable discussion for more than two decades. The name *SHAR-GA-NI-LUGAL-URU*, known from inscriptions found at Tello, Nippur, Bismya and elsewhere, was identified by Sayce, Hommel and Tiele with Sargon written *SHAR-GI-na*, followed by the king's first title *shar âli*. Pinches at first followed Ménant by reading *lugal-lag*, but later adopted *shar âli*. Oppert read *shar-imsi*, but, with Ménant, considered the element as part of the name, *i.e.*, *Shar-ga-ni-shar-imsi*. Oppert later read the name *Shar-ga-ni-shar-ali*. Hilprecht adopted this reading, and with Sayce and others considered the ruler to be identical with Sargon, explaining the name as a contraction or abbreviation of the fuller form.[1]

This reading *Shargani-shar-âli* had been until recently widely accepted, but by reason of the fact that Thureau-Dangin[2] discovered that *URU* has the value *rî*, Dhorme[3] read the characters *LUGAL URU = shar-rî*, which he considered to be part of the name.[4] Some scholars

---
[1] Cf. *Old Babylonian Inscriptions*, B. E., I, part 1, p. 16 ff.
[2] *I. S. A.*, p. 244, X, I, 2; also p. 240, II.
[3] *O. L. Z.*, 1907, p. 230.
[4] Cf. also Poebel, Z. A., XXI, p. 228, and Thureau-Dangin, *O. L. Z.*, 1908, p. 314 f.

now read the name *Shar-Gani-sharri*, some of whom considered *Gani* to be the name of a god, by reason of the identification of such a deity by Scheil.[1]

A recent find at Susa of two portions of a large monolith, published by Gautier,[2] and later by Scheil,[3] contains a cartouche in front of the king's image, in which his name is written *Sharru-GI sharru*. The name is read by these scholars "*Sharru-ukîn*, the king," the same as the name of the late Assyrian king, known to us as Sargon, who is referred to in the Old Testament; and, as mentioned above, has been regarded hitherto as the same as the supposed abbreviated form of *Shargani-shar-âli*, but to be read *Shar-Gani-sharri* or *Sharganisharri*.

Scheil[4] considered, however, *Sharru-GI* as another than *Shar-Gani-sharri*. Inasmuch as *Sharru-ukîn* in a tablet found at Tello[5] bestows upon *Narâm-Sin* the patesiship of Shirpurla, Scheil argued that they were father and son; while *Shar-Gani-sharri* he considered to be another king of Akkad belonging to the same dynasty, but who followed the other rulers. This view is also advanced by Halévy.[6]

Thureau-Dangin[7] took exception to this conclusion, because of the name *Sharru-ukîn-ili*, "Sargon is my

---

[1] *Del. en Perse*, I, p. 16, u. 3.
[2] *Rec. de trav.*, Vol. XXVII, pp. 176 f.
[3] *Del. en Perse*, X, p. 4.
[4] *Del. en Perse*, X, pp. 4 f.
[5] Cf. *Recueil de Tablettes Chaldeennes*, No. 83.
[6] *Revue Sémitique*, 1908, pp. 377 ff.
[7] *O. L. Z.*, 1908, pp. 313 f.

THE NAME OF SARGON 183

god," found on an undated tablet which he assigns to the time of Naram-Sin. The *Sharru-GI* of the text published by Gautier and Scheil he placed in the Kish dynasty, preceding the Akkad dynasty, and proposed that we have the following order of rulers of Kish: *Shar-ru-GI*, *Manishtusu*, *Uru-mu-ush*; and of Akkad, *Shar-Gani-sharri* and *Narâm-Sin*.

King[1] also considers *Sharru-GI* of the new stele, published by Gautier and Scheil, to be a still earlier king of Kish, using two texts to prove his point. In one, however, which was published by Scheil,[2] the only trace of the name is the last character $GI(?)$ at the end of the first line; which reading the author acknowledges to be doubtful. The other inscription quoted is also of a king of Kish found at Tello, of which the only part of the name that is preserved is the first sign, namely, *Sharru*. King, therefore, proposes the reading *Sharru-GI* (i.e., a deity *GI*), instead of *Sharru-kênu*, and considers that this king of Kish is not to be identified with *Shar-Gani-sharri*, the father of Naram-Sin, king of Akkad. In order to explain why in the late Assyrian and Babylonian tradition Sargon was called king of Agade or Akkad, and the father of Naram-Sin, he says, "It is clear, therefore, that the name of Sargon, king of Kish, has been borrowed for the king of Akkad, whose real name, *Shar-Gani-sharri*, has disappeared."

In short Scheil's order is: *Sharru-ukîn*, king of

---
[1] *Proceedings of the Society of Biblical Archæology*, XXX, p. 240.
[2] *Del. en Perse*, I, p. 4.

Akkad, is followed by *Narâm-Sin*, his son, and later by a certain *Shar-gani-sharri*. Thureau-Dangin and King make *Sharru-GI* a king of Kish, and *Shar-Gani-sharri*, followed by his son *Narâm-Sin*, kings of Akkad.

It is not improbable that there was another king of this era by the name of Sargon, who belonged to the dynasty of Kish, but it must be recognized that the theory advanced is exceedingly precarious, because concerning the one inscription it should be said that other rulers' names begin with *LUGAL*; and concerning the other inscription, the *GI* is so uncertain that Scheil, although when he originally published the translation of the text[1] read *Gi*(?), later[2] he did not even suggest that much. Until, therefore, more evidence is forthcoming that there was a *Sharru-GI* of the Kish dynasty, the theory that the so-called *Sharri-Gani-sharri*, the father of Naram-Sin, was credited with the achievements of the still greater predecessor, and that the confusion is to be accounted for because both were great conquerors of the same age, and that both belonged to the Semitic wave of domination and restored the Sippar temple, and because their names are not dissimilar (with which the writer differs, see below), must for the present be considered as rather questionable.

The names used by Dhorme[3] to prove that *URU* in these names following *LUGAL* is to be read *rí* are

---

[1] *Del. en Perse*, II, p. 4, note.
[2] *Saison de Fouilles à Sippar*, p. 96.
[3] *O. L. Z.*, 1907, p. 230.

THE NAME OF SARGON 185

Bi-in-ga-ni-shar-rî (otherwise known as *Bingani-shar-âli*), *U-bi-in-shar-rî* from the Manishtusu Obelisk, and *I-shir-shár-rî*.[1] The latter name is not to be regarded as a parallel writing, inasmuch as the sign used is *shár, sár*. In the other names, as well as every occurrence of the name *Shargani-LUGAL-URU*, the character in question is *LUGAL*.

Some of those who have accepted this reading see in the second element the name of a god *Gani*, by reason of the names *Ga-ni-i-li* and *Ilu-Ga-ni* which are found on the Manishtusu Obelisk. King[2] compares *Sharru-GI sharru* with *Shar-Gani-sharri*. He says there is no proof for the reading *ukîn* or *kênu* for *GI* at the time of the kingdom of Kish, and suggests that *GI* as well as *Gani* may be a deity. This name would then mean "The king is *GI*." If *sharri* is part of the name, then it cannot be the supposed "Sargon, king of Kish," since the comparison is not possible. But how can the new readings of the names *Shar-Gani-sharri* and *Bin-Gani-sharri* be translated? Dhorme[3] changes *U-bi-in-shar(LUGAL)-rî(URU)* into *Ubil-sharri*, and translates "Mon roi a apporté." *Shargani-shar-URU* he reads *Shir-ga-ni-shar-ri*, and translates "Sois juste, ô Gani, mon roi." *Bingani-shar-URU* he changes to *Bi-il-ga-ni-shar-rî*, and translates "Apporté, ô Gani, mon roi."

Such formations and names, with similar meanings, are, however, unknown in Babylonian nomenclature.

---
[1] Cf. *Rec. de Tab. Chal.*, 127, Rev. IV, 3.
[2] *P. S. B. A.*, 1908, p. 242.
[3] *Ibid.*, p. 231.

Not only is the formation and meaning peculiar, but where in this period, or in any other, does the character *LUGAL* regularly have a phonetic complement *ri* or *ru*? Or, if it is considered to be a phonogram, where in this age or in any other does *LUGAL* regularly have the phonetic value *shar*. When the scribe in the Manishtusu Obelisk wrote the name Sargon phonetically we find *Shár-ru-GI*; cf. also *Shár-ru-i-li*, *Shár-ru-dûri*, etc. In the brick inscription of Naram-Sin, published by Scheil,[1] *Shár-ru* is twice written.[2] This must be regarded not only as a serious objection to the reading, but proof that it is incorrect; for it could not be inferred that on such monuments as the Obelisk or the votive objects of Sargon, found at Nippur and Tello, or in the date formulas, or in the so-called name *Bin-Gani-sharri*, etc., we would expect such graphical expediencies or, as the Germans say, "Spielereien."[3] For these and other reasons we are, there-

---

[1] *Del. en Perse*, II, Pl. 13 : 1.

[2] Cf. also *Shár-la-ak*, king of *Kutû*, Vor. Bib., I, p. 225; *Shár-ri-ish-ta-qal*, Rev. Ass., Pl. VIII, 1897; as well as all the names compounded with *Shár-rum* in Ranke, *Personal Names*.

[3] What has been said concerning *LUGAL* also applies to the Hammurabi Code, e.g., *I-lu LUGAL URU*, III : 16, can scarcely be translated "god of kings" or "god of king." The original translation, "the divine city king," seems to be more reasonable, but perhaps not final. There is one passage, however, that seems to support the reading in the Hammurabi period. Dr. Poebel has called attention to it (cf. Z. A., XXI, p. 228). In King's *Letters*, Vol. II, No. 58, Col. II : 37, *LUGAL LUGAL E-NE-IR* is found. In text No. 57 of the same volume the Semitic translation of this text reads : *sharru in* LUGAL-URU.

fore, compelled to return to the reading *LUGAL URU*, instead of *shar-rî* or *sharri(-rî)*; and the question arises whether the combination of characters be read *Shargani-shar-âli, shargani shar âli*, or *Shar-gani LUGAL URU*?

In the light of what follows, if *LUGAL URU* is considered to be a title, it seems to me there is no difficulty whatever in identifying the traditional *Sharru-kênu* with the father of Naram-Sin, hitherto known as *Shar-ga-ni-shar-âli* and *Shar-Gani-sharri*; and at the same time all other difficulties vanish. In other words, the *Sharru-GI* of the stele published by Gautier and Scheil is the same ruler who is mentioned as bestowing the patesiship of Tello upon Naram-Sin in the texts published by Thureau-Dangin, and was the father of Naram-Sin.

The well-known tradition of Sargon in the chronicles and omen texts, as well as in the cylinder of Nabonidus, in which his name is written *Sharru-kênu*, show us: 1, that he was not of royal descent, having been reared by Akki the irrigator;[1] 2, that he was followed by Naram-Sin, who was his son; 3, that he was king of Akkad; 4, that he conquered *Amurru*; 5, and that he conquered Elam.

1. The inscription of *Shargani shar URU*, as well as the dating of tablets in his reign, show that he does not claim royal ancestry, being the son of a commoner, *Dati-Ellil*; 2, that Naram-Sin was king of this dynasty,

---

[1] *A-bi ul i-di* of the legend does not mean that he did not know his father's name, but like the personal name refers to a posthumous child.

and in all probability the son and successor of *Shargani*, especially by reason of the fact that Dr. Haynes found that the pavement laid in the temple at Nippur by Naram-Sin consisted of bricks intermingled with those of *Shargani*, as well as the fact that both by their inscriptions tell us that they were devotees of the Shamash temple at Sippar, both had the same scribe, namely, *Lugal-usum-gal*, patesi of Shirpurla, and because of the *bullæ*, referred to below, which were found at Tello; 3, that he also was king of Akkad; 4, that he conquered *Amurru*;[1] 5, and that he conquered Elam.[2]

The recently published inscription of *Shar-ru-GI* by Scheil[3] shows that he too ruled over *Shirpurla*, and that he made Naram-Sin patesi of that city. Unless it is assumed, with King, that this is another Sargon— but then we must add, who was succeeded by another Naram-Sin, and that both ruled Shirpurla, as did *Shargani* and his son—we must recognize a most peculiar combination of coincidences.

At Bismya, Banks found brick-stamps of "Naram-Sin, builder of the Temple of Nanâ," and also *bullæ* which contained the seal impression of *Shargani shar URU*. The brick-stamps are of the same general character as those found at Nippur belonging to Naram-Sin. It seems to me that inasmuch as we know that *Sharru-GI* appointed Naram-Sin as patesi of Shirpurla, and that the *bullæ* of *Shargani shar URU*, addressed to

---

[1] Cf. Thureau-Dangin, *V. B.*, I, p. 225.
[2] Cf. *ibid.*, p. 225.
[3] Cf. *Del. en Perse*, X, pp. 4 f.

Naram-Sin, have been found there, and having no other trace of a ruler Naram-Sin, we must conclude that the phonetic writing *Shar-ga-ni* represents the name written ideographically *Sharru-kênu(GI)*, and that they belong to the same person.

Scholars are practically all agreed that Sargon was a Semite. His inscriptions, as well as others belonging to the dynasty, point to the fact that it was Semitic. If a god *Gani* is to be recognized in his name, and that of his grandson, "the element" *Shar* and *Bin* would offer no difficulty. But if the supposed god *Gani* does not exist in these names, *Shargân* might be a formation on *ân* from a root שׂרג, with which, as has been done, we can compare the name of the early Hebrew patriarch Serug (written with שׂ), but especially with the name of the city *Sarugi* in the Ḫarran Census (Johns, *Deeds and Documents*, p. 72). The scribes, who wrote the name in cuneiform, could write it in two ways; that is, phonetically as they heard it, namely, *Shar-ga-ni*, and ideographically, by using ideograms which represent approximately at least the pronunciation of the name, irrespective of the meaning, namely, *Shar(ru)* (*i.e., LUGAL*) and *GI = kênu*; and yet perhaps not without consideration of the meaning, namely, "the true king," especially if the scribes had any desire of pleasing their sovereign who was a usurper. In the Assyrian period, the king who adopted this name of the illustrious ruler of early Babylonian history doubtless had in mind the meaning which the ideographic writing conveyed, namely, "the true" or "legitimate king."

There remains to be considered the usual *LUGAL URU* which follows *Shargani, Bingani,* and also the name *Ubin* of the Manishtusu Obelisk. The original explanation that it was a title, "city king," does not seem unreasonable, and much can be said in its favor. Even if *LUGAL URU* is to be explained otherwise in the Sargonic period, it is not unlikely that the title in some periods means "king of the city."

In the light of these investigations, however, and in connection with the reading for this sign when it refers to the deity of the West-land, as we have seen above, I would like to propose another possible explanation, namely, that *Uru* here means the country, and that the name and title *Shargâni shar Uru* means "Sargon, king of *Ûri.*" By this title was recognized the "suzerainty of *Ûri,*" which in the Sumerian inscriptions was written *KI-BUR-BUR = Ki-Ûri,* "Land Uru," and later in Babylonia, *Akkad* or *MAR-TU* (see below). This land *Uri* extended from what was known as *Engi* (Shumer) to the shores of the Mediterranean (see above in Part II). The fact does not seem to be ordinarily appreciated that some of the earliest rulers known by their records show that they extended their conquests over this part of Western Asia. In fact in the few inscriptions that have come down to us this stands out prominently. These expeditions were not raids for the purpose of plundering, but were for conquest, and were equal in extent, in the way of holding the lands in subjection, with those of the later periods. The omen texts, which had been re-edited in the late period, credit Sargon with the title *shar kibrat arba'im*, *i.e.*, "king of the four quarters,"[1] although there is no verification of this fact in the inscriptions of Sargon thus far published. How is this to be explained?

The inscriptions thus far known doubtless belong to the early part of his reign when he had conquered only *MARTU*, which gave him the title "king of *Ûri*" (*shar Ûri*); but in later years, by reason of certain additional conquests, he was able to assume the title which embraced a quasi-worldwide dominion; or he may have preferred the less pretentious title, even after he had accomplished this work. This can be inferred from what is written in the omen texts found in Ashurbanipal's library, which mention Elam in the East and Subartu in the North, as well as other important lands, as having been invaded. The chronicles of early kings[2] referring to Sargon say: "Afterwards in his old age all the lands revolted against him . . . . afterwards he attacked the land *Subartu* in his might," etc. They also state:[3] "Sargon, who marched against the country of the West, and conquered the country of the West, his hand subdued the [four] quarters." We have a parallel case in the reign of *Dungi*, where in the later years of his rule he conquered the "four quarters" and handed down to his successor the title, exactly as did Sargon (see below).

This title, namely, "King of the four quarters,"

---

[1] Cf. King, *Chronicles*, II, p. 27.
[2] Cf. King, *Chronicles*, II, p. 6.
[3] *Ibid.*, p. 27.

Naram-Sin inherited. In other words, the title of Naram-Sin, as well as that of Sargon in the omen texts, *i.e., shar kibrat arba'im*, was a *terminus technicus*, implying virtually a sovereignty which extended north, east, south and west of the center of the empire, which in the case of Sargon was *Akkad* (*A-GA-DE*), *i.e.*, the city Akkad as the capital. The omen texts show that the four quarters referred to were Amurru, Subartu, Elam and Accad (which doubtless included Engi).

Bingani, the son of Naram-Sin, did not, as far as we know, enjoy the title "King of the four quarters." One or more of the countries may in his day have regained independence. The title which he alone could boast of was "King of *Ûri*." *Lugal-zaggisi* and *Enshagkushanna* used the title *lugal kalamma*, "king of the world," the "dominion which extended from the lower sea of the Tigris and Euphrates (*i.e.*, the Persian Gulf) as far as the upper sea" (*i.e.*, the Mediterranean).

Ur-Engur only used the title "King of *Engi* and *Ûri*." In other words he was king over Shumer, *i.e.*, Southern Babylonia, and also the *Ûri* region, which extended from Shumer to the Mediterranean sea. His numerous references to *Amurru* and its products alone would imply that he reigned in that land. *Dungi* used the same title; but in several of his inscriptions he called himself *lugal an-ub-da tab-tab-ba*, which is the Sumerian for *shar kibrat arba'im*, "king of the four quarters." In the dates of the latter half of his reign we learn that he made notable conquests. These doubtless enabled him to use the all important and comprehensive title. This was enjoyed also by his successors, *Amar-Sin, Gimil-Sin*, and *Ibi-Sin*, the other three kings of the Ur dynasty. The kings of the Isin dynasty, as I have shown,[1] were in all probability foreigners who overthrew the preceding dynasty; and in doing so evidently lost control of Elam, or some important territory, for *Libit-Ishtar, Ishme-Dagan, Ur-NINIB, Bur-Sin* and *Sin-mâgir*, as well as *Gungunu* and *Sin-iddinam*, only used the title "King of *Engi* and *Ûri*." *Eri-Aku* and *Rim-Aku* (Sin) also used this title. *Kudur-Mabug*, their father, in several inscriptions is known as *Adda Emutbal*, "Suzerain of Emutbal," but in another he called himself also *Adda Martu*, "Suzerain of *Ûri*." Hammurabi, after his overthrow of *Rim-Aku*, as well as of Elam, became the possessor of this title, namely, "Suzerain of *Ûri*." We find him using the title "King of *Engi* and *Ûri*" and "King of the four quarters" in the same inscription. In this connection should be mentioned the statue of Hammurabi found at Diarbekir (*i.e.*, in *Urarṭu*), which contains the single title "King of *Ûri*" (*MAR-TU*), the same as used by Sargon. We recognize, therefore, three general titles besides those used in connection with the individual state or city kingdom, namely, *shar Ûri*, "King of *Ûri*," *lugal Ki-Engi Ki-Ûri*, "King of Shumer and Akkad" (*i.e.*, *Engi* and *Ûri*), and *shar kibrat arba'im* (which is the same as the Sumerian *an-ub-da tab-tab-ba*), and *lugal kalamma*.

---

[1] Cf. *Proceedings of the American Oriental Society*; cf. also Ranke, O. L. Z., Vol. 28, p. 135.

Some time after the foregoing was written and in shape for the printer, I found (February 7, 1909) in the Library Collection of Mr. J. Pierpont Morgan, of New York City, a fragment of a tablet of Sargon, which had just been shipped from England by Dr. C. H. W. Johns. Following is the transliteration of the fragment:

    A-na-ku Sha-ru-ki-in
    na-ra-am ^{d}Ishtar
    mu-te-li-ik
    ki-ib-ra-a-at
    ir-bi-ti-in
    . . mi(?)-tu-ru-ru
    . . . .

This perhaps is to be translated as follows: "I Sargon beloved of *Ishtar* a ruler(?) of the four quarters" (*i.e.*, the kingdom of the four quarters) . . . ."

The special value of this fragment is the confirmation of the view above advanced in connection with the name and titles of Sargon. Naturally, it is possible to assume that it was issued by another Sargon, who was "king of the four quarters," but, as mentioned above, the existence of such must first be proved. The fragment shows that the full name of the king was *Sharukin*; and further, that in this tablet he no longer calls himself "king of *Ûri*" (*shar Ûru*), but speaks of his kingdom as the *kibrat irbitin*,[1] which substantiates the view that after he had conquered the territory embraced in the title "King of the four quarters," he was in a position to assume it, and to hand on to his son Naram-Sin.

---

[1] Nunnation instead of mimmation.

IV. THE NAME NIN-IB

In publishing the Archives of the Murashû Sons of Nippur, in 1904, the writer found a large number of documents which contained short reference notes, called in legal parlance "endorsements." These reference notes were scratched or written with ink on the tablet in the Aramaic language for the benefit of the archive keeper.[1] On several of these tablets were found names which were compounded with the name of the deity *NIN-IB*, e.g., *NINIB-iddina*. But instead of finding anything like what had been proposed, namely, Adar, Nindar, Ninrag, Nin-Urash and Nisroch, there was written in each instance אנושת. Before finding an additional tablet which contained the Aramaic equivalent, there seemed to be some doubt whether the middle character should be read ר or ו, although preference was given to the latter. Another example, however, was found which confirmed the preferred reading.

The result of the discovery of this Aramaic equivalent, instead of solving the problem, seemed to make the obscurity which surrounded the pronunciation

---

[1] See Clay, *Babylonian Expedition*, Vol. X, pp. 5 f.; *Light on the Old Testament from Babel*, p. 394, and "Aramaic Endorsements on the Documents of the Murashû Sons," *Harper Memorial Volume*, I, pp. 289 f., and "The Origin and Real Name of *NIN-IB*," *J. A. O. S.*, 1907.

still denser. The writer at the same time had several theories in mind with reference to the vocalization and meaning of the characters, but none were published, as they did not seem sufficiently satisfactory. Some of these, however, have been published by others.[1]

---

[1] The interesting collection of views on the Aramaic equivalent and the interpretations of it which follow shows how diversified has been the understanding of scholars. Professor Hilprecht, in his editorial preface to my *Murashû* texts (*i.e., B. E.*, Vol. X), as well as in an article in *The Sunday School Times*, September 25, 1904, took exception to my reading and read two characters differently, *i.e.*, אנרשח. In explaining the name he proposed comparison with *NIN-SHAH*, "Lord of the Boar" = the Syriac נארשג, and regarded it identical with the biblical Nisroch, in whose temple at Nineveh Sennacherib worshiped. The Syriac form, however, is נאריג (cf. Jastrow, *Rel. Bab. und Ass.*, Vol. I, p. 451), which of course makes the comparison impossible. Further, the final character of the Aramaic of *NIN-IB* is not ח but ת, as I had maintained, and which has since been proved correct. The reading of ר instead of ו inspired a series of other readings which follow. Professor Zimmern, as quoted by Professor Hilprecht in *The Sunday School Times* (September 25, 1904), read *blprsht* = *bêl pirishti*, "Lord of decision." Professor Prince, in the *Journal of Biblical Literature* (vol. 1905, p. 55), followed in reading *Enu rêshtu*, "The chief lord." Dr. Pinches, about the same time, in the *Journal of the Royal Asiatic Society* (January, 1905), read *En-rêsheth* = *Enu rêshtu*, "The primæval lord." Professor Johns, *Expository Times* (December, 1904), p. 141, read *Urashtu*, and on p. 141, *ibid.*, *Arashtu*. Professor Sayce, in the same journal (December, 1904), regarded it as equivalent to the Assyrian *In-arishti*, "Lord of the mitre," the Sumerian for *Nin-Urash*. In the *Revue Sémitique* (1905, p. 93), Professor Halévy offered the reading *En napishti*, "Lord of life," or preferably *En-nawashti* = *En-nammashti*, "seigneur de tout ce qui est doué de vie de mouvement, de toute creature animée." Later (cf. *ibid.*, p. 180), the same scholar offered two other explanations: *en-rishati*, "seigneur de

Besides Jensen and Halévy, of those who have published their views, Lidzbarski is the only scholar who accepted my reading.[1] In an article on "The Origin and Real Name of *NIN-IB*," which appeared in the *Transactions of the American Oriental Society*, Vol. XXVIII, p. 135, the writer, holding that the middle character is unmistakably ו, not ד, proposed the formula אנושת = *En-mashtu* = *En-martu* = *Ba'al-Amurru* (see below). Since this publication appeared, Hrozny[2] read the characters *In-nummashtu* = *nammashshu* from *numushda*.

In the early spring of last year a potsherd from Nippur, which had been classified as a fragment of a Hebrew bowl, proved in the skillful hands of my colleague, Professor Montgomery, to be an ostracon, on which the name is written in Aramaic no less than five times.[3] It put the reading of the Aramaic beyond cavil, showing that my own from the very first was correct.

The explanation that I have advanced, namely, that the Aramaic אנושת for *NIN-IB* was a reproduction of the Sumerian *EN-MAR-TU*, the lord *par excellence* of the West-land, does not seem to me to have been

---

l'allégresse," and *en-arishti*, "seigneur du vêtement princier nommé *arishtu*." Professor Jensen (*Gilgamesh Epos*, p. 87) read and interpreted the character *enwusht* = *namushtu* = *namurtu*, with which he compared the biblical Nimrod. Three other explanations were sent me in private communications: *Irrishtu*, the feminine of *Irrishu*, "farmer"; *en erishti*, "Lord of decision," and an identification with the Persian word for the planet Saturn, *nivishti ḫudâ*, "the prescience of god," or *nuwashtan*, "to go far away."

[1] Cf. *Ephemeris*, Vol. II, p. 203.
[2] *Revue Semitique*, July, 1908.
[3] See *Jour. Amer. Or. Soc.*, 1908, p. 204.

improved upon. For the change of *r* to *sh*, compare *martum (TUR-SAL)* = *mashtum*, "daughter" (Jensen, Z. A., IV, p. 436), *shipishti* for *shipirti* in the Murashû Documents; the Neo-Babylonian personal name *Mashtuku*, written *Martuku* in the Cassite period; also the deity *Ashka'iti* = *Arka'iti*, and the article by Jensen, Z. A., VII, p. 179. For an exact parallel to the *EN-MARTU* = *Bêl-Amurru* cf. *EN-KAS* = *Bêl-Ḫarran*, in the name index of Johns, *Deeds and Documents*, and *Doomsday Book*; but especially *DINGIR-MAR-TU*, "the deity of *Amurru*." In arguing for an Amorite origin of *NIN-IB*, or, better expressed, that it represented a deity of Amurru, as others had done,[1] reference was made to the West Semitic name *Abdi-NIN-IB*, the city *ᵃˡᵘNIN-IB* according to the collation of Knudtzon,[2] and the name of a place or temple in or near Jerusalem (*i.e.*, in the district of the city) called *Bît-NIN-IB*.[3] In the same paper it was suggested that *NIN-IB* was originally the chief goddess *Ba'alat Amurru*, which perhaps was *Ashtarti*; and that at some center in Babylonia, probably Dilbat, the deity appeared as the consort of *IB*, who later was known as *Urash*. In other words, the theory is that the god of the West, when introduced at a certain center in Babylonia, was written by the Sumerian chirographers *IB*, which conveyed to them

---

[1] Cf. Zimmern, *K. A. T.*³, p. 411.
[2] Cf. *B. A.*, IV, p. 114.
[3] Cf. *K. B.*, V.

THE NAME NIN-IB 199

the idea represented by the Western solar deity;[1] and his consort's name, probably Ashtarti, was written *NIN-IB*.[2] Later, as was the case in so many instances when *NIN-IB* became masculinized,[3] in certain quarters the deity was regarded as the "Lord" *par excellence* of Amurru, *i.e.*, *Ba'al Amurru*, when the Sumerian equivalent *EN-MAR-TU*, "Lord *Amurru*," was introduced. And this Sumerian form, like *EN-LIL*, was handed down into later times, as the Aramaic form of the name shows. Of course, it is not necessary to waste space in showing how *EN-MAR-TU*, like *EN-LIL*, could pass into Babylonian as *Enwashtu* and *Ellil*, and be reproduced in Aramaic as אנושת and אלל.

Another theory concerning the reading and understanding of the name by the help of the Aramaic now becomes more plausible. In discussing the name Gilga-Mesh it became apparent that the name is West Semitic, written in Sumerian, and that it perhaps contains the name of the mountain god *Mash*, which is to be identified with *Mash* (מש) of Genesis 10 : 23. It was further shown that in Nineveh there was a temple *E-MASH-MASH*, which is written *E-MISH-*

---

[1] It is interesting to note that Zimmern (*K. A. T.*[3], p. 411), in discussing *Bît-NIN-IB* of Jerusalem, as against Haupt (Joshua, *Poly. Bib.*, p. 54), who says that *NIN-IB* represents Yahweh, assumes among the other possibilities that it may be a designation of a native deity, Shamash or El.

[2] It is not improbable that *NIN-MAR*, the name of the deity in Girsu, of whom Ur-Nina, Dungi and others were patrons, represents the same god; cf. also the personal name $Ur\text{-}^{d}NIN\text{-}MAR^{ki}$ (*V. B.*, I, pt. 1, p. 148, No. 21).

[3] Cf. Barton, *Semitic Origins*.

MISH in the Ḫammurabi Code; and also that the temple of the West Semitic Nergal at Cutha is called *E-MISH-LAM*, and that the temple at Agade is called *E-UL-MASH*. The element was also shown to be in the names *Di-Mash-qi, Karke-Mish*, etc. (see Part II).

In Bezold's *Catalogue of the Kouyunjik Collection*,[1] and in Brünnow's Classified List, No. 1778, the following formula is found:

Ma-ash | MASH | ma-a-shu | ^{d}*NIN-IB*

This considered in connection with the ideogram *MASH*, which was commonly used in writing the name of the deity, becomes especially interesting. Then also in Bezold's *Catalogue*[2] the following is written:

^{d}*Ma-a-shu u* ^{d}*Ma-ash-tum mârê Sin.*
"The god *Mâshu* and *Mâshtum* children of *Sin.*"

Mâshtu, therefore, was originally the feminine of *Mâsh*. *NIN-IB* originally was feminine and later became masculinized (see above). In a group of gods given in connection with their consorts in Harper's *Letters*,[3] *NIN-IB* follows *NIN-IB* as if his counterpart,[4] which very likely is due to the fact that at that time the god and his consort bore one and the same name. This change in sex naturally points to a misunderstanding at some time. *NIN-IB* therefore could be regarded

---

[1] K., 7790, , p. 875.
[2] It is of course not impossible that NIN-IB is a mistake for Gula.
[3] K., 6335, p. 81.
[4] Vol. IV, No. 358.

as equivalent to *Mâshtu*. *EN-Mâshtu*, *i.e.*, *EN*, "lord," and *Mâshtu*, the god[dess], may have arisen in such a center as Nippur, where the deity became one of the patron gods of the city; that is, after the feminine *Mâshtu* had become masculinized the deity was called "Lord *Mâshtu*," like *LUGAL-Urra*, "King or Lord *Ûra*," etc. This explanation I now regard preferable, but it is to be noted that both identify the deity with the West.

V. THE NAME YAHWEH

WITH the discovery of the name Yahweh in the cuneiform literature, exclusive of proper names, under the form $Jâwu(m)$ (see page 89), the question arises whether it throws any light on the ancient pronunciation of the divine name.

Before the discovery of the Aramaic papyri at Assuan, certain scholars claimed that Yahweh is identical with the Canaanitic deity $Jâhû$, which they said is found in Ja-u-$ḫa$-zi, Ja-u-bi-'-di, etc. Since the discovery of the Assuan papyri,[1] in which יהו occurs for the divine name, it seems that scholars generally have adopted the reading $Jâhû$. This conclusion, however, cannot be maintained.

In a former work I endeavored to show[2] that the divine name of the pre-Christian period was practically identical with the pronunciation which Theodoret informs us he obtained from the Samaritans, namely 'Ιαβε, which is also found in a Samaritan letter in Arabic to de Sacy,[3] namely, $Jahwa$ or $Jahwe$, and the pronunciation which has been accepted for years, namely $Jahweh$. This, as has been claimed, is preserved

---

[1] See Sachau, *Aramäische Papyrusurkunden*, p. 25. "Die Juden in Elephantin nannten ihren Gott nicht יהוה sondern יהו, wofür ich nach Vorgang der Assyrer die Aussprache $Jâhû$ annehme."

[2] *Light on the Old Testament from Babel*, p. 247f.

[3] See Montgomery, *Journal of Biblical Literature*, XXV, 1906, p. 50.

in *Jâwa* (*Ja-a-ma*),[1] an element in Jewish names in the Neo-Babylonian period[2] and in *Jâwu*(*m*) on the tablet in the Morgan Library Collection (see p. 89), and on one in the possession of Professor Delitzsch, which came from the same source.

The chief objection to the pronunciation *Jâhû* is to be found in the writing יהוה, the Old Testament form of the name, which also occurs on the Moabite stone. Can it be said that the Hebrew writers in Israel and Moab did not know how to write the divine name? What does the additional final letter mean? Did they add it to obscure the pronunciation? Or, did the Jews pronounce the name one way in Palestine, and another way in Egypt, and still another way in Babylonia? The writer maintains that יהוה, יהו, as well as *Jâwu* (*Jâwi* and *Jâwa*), all represent the same pronunciation; and, as above, that this pronunciation is preserved in the Greek 'Ιαβε, in the Arabic *Jahwe*, and in the accepted modern transcription *Jahwe* or *Jahweh*.

As the first element in personal names, Yahweh occurs in the Assyrian historical inscriptions as *Ja-u*, in *Ja-u-ḫazi* and *Ja-u-bi'di;* and in the Neo-Babylonian period as *Ja-ḫu-u*, *Ja-a-ḫu-u* and *Ja-a-ḫu* in *Ja-ḫu-u-natannu*, etc.[3] Perhaps also it is to be found in *Ja-u-*

---

[1] See Clay, *Light on the Old Testament from Babel*, p. 248.

[2] Pinches, *Proc. Soc. Bib. Arch.*, XV, 13ff., was the first to call attention to these names.

[3] See Clay, *B. E.*, Vol. X, p. 19, and *Light on the Old Testament from Babel*, p. 241 f.

bâni of the Cassite period,[1] and in *Jaum-El* of the Hammurabi period (see below).

As the second element in personal names it occurs in *Ashirat-Ja-wi* in the Hammurabi period of *V.* S, VII 157 : 7, and in *Aḫi-Ja-mi* (*Ja-wi*) of the Ta'annek tablet; and in the Assyrian historical inscriptions as *Ja-a-u* and *Ja-u* in *Ḫazaqi-Ja-a-u*, etc., in the Gezer tablet in *Natan-Ja-u*, also in the Neo-Babylonian tablets as *Ja-a-ma* (*Jâwa*), in *Natannu-Ja-a-ma*, etc.[2] It is not improbable that it occurs also in other forms, as in *Ḫa-an-ni-ja*, etc., which, owing to their uncertainty, are not included in the discussions.[3]

Assuming that *Jâwu(m)* of the early period, the only form known where in cuneiform it is not compounded with other elements, represents the divine name, it can be shown that the same pronunciation also represents the element when written in the Hebrew script.

The form יהו as the first element, when reproduced in cuneiform in the Assyrian period, became *Ja-u*, where the *h* between the two vowels was elided; and in the Neo-Babylonian period it became *Ja-ḫu-u*, *Ja-a-ḫu* and *Ja-a-ḫu-u*, where the *h* is represented by the Babylonian *ḫ*. The explanation of the Massoretic יְהוֹ usually offered is the one proposed by the late Professor Franz Delitzsch,[4] namely: יְהוֹ = יָהוּ = יָהוּ. It seems to me

---

[1] See Clay, *B. E.*, Vol. XV, p. 32.
[2] See *Light on the Old Testament*, p. 244.
[3] On these, see Jastrow, *Journal of Biblical Literature*, XIV, p. 108 ff., and Daiches, *Zeit. für Ass.*, XXII, p. 125 ff.
[4] See *Z. A. W.*, II, 173 f.; 280 ff.

that the origin of the form יְהוֹ is to be found in יָהְוֻ, which was the full name; and that *Jahwu-natan* became *Jahû-natan* or *Jahô-natan*. The consonant *w* followed by a homogeneous vowel, owing to the secondary accent falling on the syllable, quiesced, like יְקוּם = יְקוּם.

The element appearing in the second place is not so difficult to explain. Prof. Franz Delitzsch claimed that יְהוּ = יְחָן which became יָהּ. It appears to me that the formula should be יְהֹן = יָהְן, which became יָהּ, the final consonant being syncopated. The ending *Jau* in the Assyrian period can be said to reproduce יָהְן; that is, the *u* may have been sounded like the semiconsonant *w*. The element is also represented in the Neo-Babylonian *Jâwa*.

The identification of *Jâwa* made originally by Pinches was accepted by other scholars, who seemed to think that *Jâwa* represented the full name. Prof. Jastrow[1] took the view that *Jâma* was an emphatic affirmative. In opposing the writer's view on the subject Prof. Hilprecht accepted[2] that of Prof. Jastrow; but the latter has since abandoned the explanation by reason of the many examples in the Murashû texts.

In the first place it has been conclusively shown that *Jâma*[3] is the divine name. Concerning the form of the writing, two possible explanations seem plausible. The first would follow those who hold that it represents the

---

[1] *Journal of Biblical Literature*, XIII, p. 101 ff., Z. A., X, p. 222 f., and Z. A. T. W., XVI, p. 1 ff.

[2] See Editorial Preface to my *B.E.*, X, p. xv, also Daiches, Z. A., XXII, p. 128 ff.

[3] Clay, *Light on the Old Testament*, p. 242 f.

206 AMURRU HOME OF NORTHERN SEMITES

uncontracted name, in which case, however, a reason must be given why it is not apocopated, inasmuch as the element in Hebrew names is always shortened. This is also shown by the Septuagint. My own suggestion[1] is that the Babylonian scribes recognized the element as the name of the Hebrew god, and that in their schools they were taught to write the full name of the deity when it appeared as the second element in names. The name, therefore, was not written as they heard it, but, as they treated their own Babylonian names, according to fixed rules. When we consider that Hebrew names compounded with *Jâma* occur more frequently in the Murashû documents than Babylonian names compounded with their own prominent deities, such as Addu, Bau, Ea, etc., we can readily understand that this could be an adopted orthography. Of the twenty-five or more different names compounded with *Jâma*, some of which occur very often, there is not a single variation from the form *Ja-a-ma;* and in every instance it is without the determinative for deity. An illustration of such an adopted writing is to be seen in *AN-MESH* or *ilu^{pl}*, which represents the West Semitic אל.[2]

Another and perfectly reasonable theory is that either the final vowel of *Jâma* was not pronounced distinctly, but as a light overhanging vowel like *Jâw^a;* or it was not pronounced at all, like *Jâw*. In other words, *Jâwa* or *Jâw(a)* stands for the apocopated form of the divine name *Jâhwu*. This apocopation or shortening

---

[1] *Light on the Old Testament*, p. 247.
[2] See Clay, *Old Testament and Semitic Studies*, I, p. 316.

of the final vowel was due to the emphasis being placed on the first syllable of the divine name, *e.g.*, *Natan-Jáhwu* became *Natan-Jahw(u)*.

Such an explanation also accounts for the change to יה, so commonly found in the Old Testament, and in the Assuan papyri, the final *w* being apocopated. It should be added that the Massoretic pointing, while possible according to phonetic laws, is not supported by the Septuagint, which usually transliterates this ending ιας. It would appear, therefore, that יהוה as well as יהו were pronounced *Jahwu(e,a)*; and that this pronunciation was in use as early as the Hammurabi period. Furthermore, Yahweh being probably of Aramæan origin, יהו may be the Aramæan form of the name, inasmuch as the Assuan papyri are written in Aramaic.

These conclusions necessitate the reconsideration of such names as *Ja-'-wi-ilu*[1] and *Ja-wi-ilu*, which Sayce, Delitzsch and others have regarded as containing the divine name. These names, as is well known, can also be read *Ja'pi-El*. In addition to the fact that there is not a single instance in the Hebrew literature where the name Yahweh remained unchanged when appearing as a first element in proper names, the West Semitic name *Ja-pa-El*,[2] also of the Hammurabi period, makes it quite reasonable that the reading should be *Ja'pi* or *Japi* instead of *Ja'wi* or *Jawi;* and that the stem of the element is probably חפה, "to cover." The name could

---

[1] Cf. *C.T.*, VIII, 20, 314:3, and VIII, 34, 544 : 4; and Ranke, *B.E.*, VI, 1, 17 : 38.

[2] Ungnad, *V. S.*, 5, VIII, 16 : 39.

be translated, as has been stated, "God has covered, protected." On the other hand, the name *Ja-u-um-El*, belonging to the early period, probably represents the divine name, because the element appears in the shortened form exactly as found in later periods.[1]

---

[1] *Light on the Old Testament*, p. 237.

INDEX

A-ba-ra-ma, 86, 170
Abdi-Ashirta, 152
Abdi-NINIB, 198
Abel-Beth-Maacah, 60
Abram, 89, 90
Abraham, 14, 40, 58, 85
Adad, 38, 48, 87, 88, 131
Adad-nirari III, 98
Adad-Teshup, 79
Adam, 43
Adapa, 64
Addu-taqummu, 101
Adoni-Zedek, 154
Agade, 79, 192
A-gar-Til-la, 103
Aelian, 78
Aḫi-Jâwi, 206
Akkad, 97, 192
Aku, 111
A-KUR-GAL, 113
Alap, 64
Alaporus, 63, 64, 158
Alap-Uru, 64
Alashia, 38
Alexander Polyhistor, 66
A-li-ba-ni-shu, 112
Almelon, 63
Al-Nashḫu-milki, 158
Aloros, 63
Al-Si', 158
Amal, 65
Amar, 95, 116
A-ma-ra, 28, 29
Amar-a-pa, 101
Amar-na-ta-nu, 101
Amar-ra-pa, 101
Amar-sha-al-ti, 101
Amar-Sin, 118, 193
A-ma-ru, 107, 117, 119
Amar-uduk, 92, 95, 120

Amegalarus, 63
amêlu, 64
Amêl-Aruru, 65
Amêl-Sin, 66
Amêl-Uru, 65
A-me-ir-rum, 106
Amemphsinus, 63
'amîr, 107
'amîrî, 107
Ammenon, 63
Ammi-ditana, 98
Ammon, 98
Amqi, 151
Amraphel, 111
Amur, 100
A-mu-ra, 28, 97
A-mur-Ashur, 161
Amur-ḫaḫa, 102
Amur-ilu, 161
A-mur-Ishtar, 161
Amurra, 97
A-mur-ri-qa-nu, 119
Amurru, 101, passim
Amurru-natannu, 102
Amurru-nazabi, 102
Amurru-shama, 102
A-mur-sa-nu, 120
A-mur-Shamash, 161
A-mur-si-gu, 120
A-mur-tin-nu, 119
Anammelek, 143
A-na-at-da-la-ti, 143
'*Anath*, 143
'*Anathoth*, 143
Aner, 143
AN-MESH, 208
An-ram, 143
Antum, 142
Anu, 142
Anu-banini, 143

Anu-ram, 144
Apsu, 47, 53
Arabia, 24, 77, 83
Arad-Sin, 110
Arallu, 77
Aram, 24
Aram-Damascus, 179
Ararat, 75
Ardata, 67
Arfa-Kesed, 170
Argaman, 104, 120
Ari, 13, 104
Arpad, 180
Arpadda(u), 180
Artaxerxes I, 68
Aruru, 64
Ashbel, 123
Asher, 65
Ashera, 140
Ashirat-Jawi, 206
Ashirta, 38
A-shir-ma-lik, 139
Ashtarti, 198, 199
Ash-tar-Til-la, 103
Ashur, 138
Ashurbanipal, 17, 46, 53, 54, 59, 60, 98
Astrology, 15
Athtara, 141
Augustine, 51
Aures, 43
Aurus, 69
Awa-ar-i-lum, 120
Awa-ar-ka-ṣir, 120
Awa-ar-sa-na-bu, 120
Awa-ar-si-qir, 120
awâtu, 105
awêlu, 105
Awîl-Ishtar, 171
A-wi-lu-tim, 106
A-wi-ir-tum, 106
Aziru, 152

Ba'al, 38
Babel, 91
Babylon, 142
Baethgen, F., 128
Banks, E. J., 114, 142, 188

Bar-iksu, 145
Barsip, 174
Barton, George A., 13, 17, 43, 44, 83, 114, 124, 141, 151, 169, 199
Bau, 38
Bayt-sha-ra, 127
Beirut, 76
Bêl, 20, 37, 47, 102
Bêl-Ḫarran, 198
Benhadad, 87
Berosus, 63, 68, 170
Bêth-'Anath, 143
Bêth-Dagan, 146
Bethel, 128
Bêth-Leḥem, 147
Bêth-sha-El, 127
Bethshean, 128
Bêth-Shemesh, 125
Bethuel, 172
Bezold, Carl, 200
Bi-in-ga-ni-shar-ri, 185
Bilga-Mish, 79
BIL-LIL, 113, 114
Bilaqqu, 79
Bir-Adad, 123
Bir-Hadad, 132
Bir-napishtim, 80, 134
Bir-napishtim-uṣur, 80
Bismaya, 142
Bît-NIN-IB, 198
Bît-Yakin, 170
Bork, F., 103
Brockelmann, Carl, 84
Brown, Francis, 163, 164
Brünnow, Rudolph, 115, 117, 120, 123, 200
Buhl, Franz, 163
BU(SIR)-NE-NE, 119, 133
BUR-BUR, 102, 113
BUR-BUR-DA, 112
Bur-Sin, 118, 193
Buzur-KUR-GAL, 82
Buzur-Ûru, 82
Byblos, 157

Cain, 65
Cappadocian tablets, 37, 39, 43

INDEX 211

Carmel, 87
Champollion, 29
Chedorlaomer, 98
Constantia, 103
Cooke, G. A., 27, 123, 157, 160, 178
Cory, 52
Craig, J. Alexander, 139
Cutha, 115
Cyrus, 38, 98

Dagan, 38, 146
Daiches, Samuel, 206, 207
Damascus, 126, 128, 130
Darius II, 68
Dati-Ellil, 67, 187
David, 17
Da(v)onus, 63
Delattre, A. J., 99
Delitzsch, Franz, 206, 207
Delitzsch, Friedrich, 36, 37, 49, 57, 71, 80, 89, 105, 107, 119, 120, 125, 128, 161, 205, 209
Der, 130
de Sacy, 204
Dhorme, P., 123, 184, 185
Dhu'l Ḥalasa, 128
Dhu'l Shara, 128
Diarbekir, 97, 98, 103, 193
Dilbat, 198
Dillmann, A., 72, 167
DI-Marduk, 116
Di-mash-qi, 79, 129, 200
Dim-mas-qa, 130
Driver, S. R., 44, 162
DUMU-URU, 110
Dungi, 97, 118, 128, 192
dûr, 130

Ea, 47, 53
Ea-bâni, 81
Ebed-Urash, 123
Ed-Deir, 147
Edom, 98
Edoranchus, 63, 69
Egyptian, 32
Ehud, 17
Elam, 97

El-Elyon, 158
Eliezer, 40, 129
Ellil, 37, 47, 48, 56, 95, 117
Ellil-bâni, 39
ellu, 107
Elohim, 124
El-Shaddai, 127, 158
Elul, 57, 59
El-Ur, 64, 158
E-MASH-MASH, 78, 126, 199
E-MISH-MISH, 78
E-MISH-LAM, 78
Emutbal, 97
Engi, 13
EN-GI-DU, 81
EN-KI-DU, 81
EN-MAR-TU, 121
EN-Mâshtu, 121, 122
En-me-dur-an-ki, 66
En-na-Zu-in, 146
Enoch, 66, 69
Enosh, 64
Enshagkushanna, 192
Envâshtu, 199
Erebus, 52
Erech, 76, 78, 126, 142
Ereshkigal, 33
Eri, 177
Eria, 112
Eri-Aku, 193
Eridu, 45, 47, 53
Esh-ba'al, 123
Eshu, 38
Ethiopic language, 83
eṭimmu, 51
Etruscans, 23
Ezekiel, 163
E-UL-MASH, 71, 126
E-UL-LAM, 78
Eupolemus, 168
Eusebius, 52

Galilee, 60
GAL-UR-RA, 113
gamâru, 56
Gar, 151
Gautier, 182, 183
gemini, 16

Gezer, 24
Gideon, 17
Gilead, 60
Gilgamesh, 50, 73, 74, 76, 77, 79, 81, 122, 126, 129
Gimil-Anim, 143
Gimil-Sin, 96, 193
GIR-URU, 110
GISH-BIL-GA, 79
GISH-BIL-GA-MISH, 78
GISH-TU-MASH, 78
Gray, G. B., 164
Greeks, 22
Grimme, H., 145, 158
Gubla, 152
Gudea, 31, 97, 103, 120, 128, 136, 180, 193
Gula, 38, 200
Gungunu, 193
Gunkel, H., 36, 44, 51, 55, 71, 72, 73

Hagar, 40
Halevy, J., 42, 107, 182, 197
Ḫalia, 140
Ḫaligalbat, 140
Ḫali-Jaum, 90
Ḫalili, 140
Ḫallu, 140
Hamath, 157
Hammurabi, 40, 41, 46, 59, 78, 79, 89, 97, 98, 107, 111, 116, 117, 186, 193
Ḫana, 147
Ḫa-an-ni-ia, 206
Haran, 16
Haran Census, 145
Harper, R. F., 124, 180, 200
Hastings, James, 151, 162, 167
Hauḫam, 154
Haupt, Paul, 80, 115, 141, 176, 199
ḫawiru, 105
Haynes, J. H., 188
Hazor, 60
Hebron, 154
Hehn, J., 56
Hermon, 126

Herodotus, 35, 142
Hilprecht, H. V., 43, 78, 118, 124, 132, 159, 181, 207
Hinke, W. J., 112
ḫirtu, 106
Hittite, 32
Hoham, 154
Hommel, F., 30, 63, 65, 66, 77, 78, 80, 84, 118, 139, 141, 154, 161, 178, 179, 181
Horeb, 87
Hrozny, F., 197
Huber, P. E., 109, 110, 111, 112
Ḫu-di-ib-Til-la, 103

IB, 38
ibbu, 107
Ibgatum, 106
Ibi-Sin, 193
Igur-kapkapu, 140
iḫîr, 106
Ijon, 60
Ikûn-pî-Ûru, 113
ilî, 124
Il-Teḫiri-abi, 158
Il-yapi'a, 154
Ilu-arapa, 101
IM-MAR-TU, 100
imtût, 105
inûḫ, 105
I-ri-ir-Til-la, 103
'*Ir-Marduk*, 176
'*Ir-Naḫash*, 176
'*Ir-Shemesh*, 176
Irushalim, 176
Ishbi-Urru, 110
I-shir-shar-ri, 185
Ishme-Dagan, 146, 193
Ishtar, 16, 38, 141
Ishtar-ki-Til-la, 103
Ishum, 133
Isin dynasty, 96
I-ti-Da-gan, 147

Jabni-El, 178
Jacob, 18
Jahû, 86
Ja-ḫu-u, 205

INDEX

Jahweh, 104
Jâma, 104, 206
Janoah, 60
Ja'pi-El, 209
Jarmuth, 154
Joseph-el, 178
Jastrow, Jr., Morris, 21, 22, 23, 26, 27, 31, 44, 46, 47, 71, 74, 80, 107, 114, 132, 206, 207
Ja-ash-bi-i-la, 110
Ja-u-ba-ni, 206
Ja-u-ḫa-zi, 204
Jaum, 90
Ja-u-um-El, 210
Jaw, 20
Ja'wi-ilu, 89
Ja-wu-um, 89, 90, 204
Jensen, Peter, 18, 19, 48, 55, 77, 78, 80, 99, 114, 115, 116, 117, 118, 128, 131, 142, 197, 198
Jeremias, A., 18, 63, 64, 65, 79, 80
Jezreel, 178
Johns, C. H. W., 58, 59, 60, 89, 100, 145, 158, 159, 160, 172, 189, 194, 198
Jonah, 53
Joppa, 53

Kadashman-Enlil, 37
KA-GAL-AD-KI, 129
Karke-Mish, 200
Kedesh, 60
Kenites, 34, 90
Kesed, 170
Khatti, 98
KI-BUR-BUR, 190
Kikia, 140
King, L. W., 112, 183, 184, 186, 191
Kiryatharba, 16
Kish, 89
Kittel, Rudolph, 167, 172
Knudtzon, J. A., 37
Kudur-Mabug, 11, 97, 193
Kugler, Franz, 21
KUR-GAL, 88, 102
KUR-GAL-êrish, 102
KUR-MAR-TU, 99

La'ash, 157
Laban, 172
Lachish, 24
Laḫâmu, 53, 147
Laḫmu, 147
Lamech, 66
Langdon, Stephen, 143
Larsa, 110, 138
Layard, Henry, 103
Leander, Pontus, 118
Libit-Ishtar, 96, 193
Lidzbarski, Mark, 24, 144, 155, 157, 158, 159, 160, 178, 197
lillu, 52
Lînûḫ-libbi-Ellil, 56
Lînuḫ-libbi-ilâni, 56
Lîpush-Jaum, 90
Little Zab, 75
Lot, 14
Lugal-kisalsi, 114
LUGAL-Urra, 38, 116, 201
Lugal-zaggisi, 192
Lyon, D. G., 153

Macalister, Alexander, 153
Macalister, Stewart, 24, 28, 153, 155
Malik, 134
Malik-ZI-NI-SU, 134
Malki-Zedek, 154
Manishtusu, 146
Mar, 95, 100
Mar-bi'di, 100
Marchesvan, 57, 59
Mardin, 103
Marduk, 20, 36, 37, 38, 44, 45, 46, 48, 49, 57, 95, 101, 116, 118
Mar-eriqqu, 120
Mar-irrish, 100
MAR-KI, 116
Mar-larimme, 100
Mar-pa-da-ai, 180
Mar-ṣuri, 100
MAR-TU, 77, 97, 99, 100, 113
MAR-TU-êrish, 102
Martuku, 198
MASH, 78, 107, 199

MASH-MASH, 38
Mashtuku, 198
Mâshtum, 198, 200, 201
Mâshu, 38, 10, 126, 128, 200
Megiddo, 24, 27
Meinhold, J., 56
Meissner, Bruno, 81, 103, 105, 107, 115, 173, 179
Menant, J., 181
Menes, 30
MESH, 78
Mesheq, 129, 131
Methû-Salah, 66
Methû-sha-El, 66, 127
Me-Tilla, 103
Meyer, Eduard, 54, 96, 97
Mil-ki-U-ri, 134, 156
Milkûru, 102
Mî-sha-El, 127
MISH, 78
Mish(?)-ki-Til-la, 103
Mitanni, 32, 38, 43
Moab, 98
Montgomery, James A., 50, 121, 157, 162, 197, 204
Moore, G. A., 23, 134
Morgan Library Collection, 28, 43, 51, 73, 80, 88, 89, 114, 194, 205
Moriah, 87
Mosaic Code, 41
Moses, 17
Mt. Niṣir, 75
Mt. Sinai, 145
Muqayyar, 167, 168
Müller, D. H., 180
Müller, W. Max, 29, 30, 127, 157
Murik-Tidnum, 96
Mur-ar-na-tim, 120
Mur-babillu, 120
MUR-ibni, 134
Mur-nisqi, 120
Mur-siparru, 120
Muss-Arnolt, W., 79, 80, 107, 112, 120, 141
Mutû-sha-Irkhu, 66

Nabonidus, 98
Nabû, 144

Nabû-idri, 144
Nabû-napishtim-uṣur, 80
Nabû-rapa, 144
Naḫarâu, 172
Naḫirî, 172
Naḫrima, 151
namâru, 107
Namratum, 106
Namtar, 33
Nanâ, 38
Nannar, 97, 169
Naphtali, 60
Naram-Sin, 115
Nashḫi, 132
nawâru, 105
Nebuchadrezzar, 68, 98
Nergal, 33, 37, 38, 114, 115, 117, 121, 126, 133
NE-URU-GAL, 95, 115, 119
Nielsen, 60
Nikkal, 95
NIN-GAL, 95
Nin-gir-su, 146
Nin-Girsu, 48, 131
NIN-IB, 37, 38, 89, 121, 126, 178
NIN-IB-iddina, 195
NIN-NE-URU(UNU), 115
NIN-MAR, 199
Ninrag, 195
Nippur, 47
Nisin, 97
Nisin dynasty, 95
Nisroch, 195
NITA, 113
Noah, 76
Nöldeke, Theodore, 47
Nowack, W., 26
nu-uḫ, 55, 76, 80
Nuḫashshi, 129
Nûḫ-libbi-ilâni, 56
Nûḫ-napishtim, 80
numushda, 197
Nushku, 37, 132

Og, 154
Olmstead, A. T., 103
Omri, 98

INDEX   215

Oppert, J., 181
Oros, 69
Otiartes, 64

pa-la-qu, 79
Paran, 87
Paton, L. B., 13
Pedaiah, 140
Pedahel, 140
Peiser, Felix, 102
Pepy, 30
Per, 80
Petrie, F., 29, 30
Philistia, 98
Phœnicia, 98
Pinches, T. G., 37, 46, 54, 78, 103, 110, 119, 125, 161, 167, 176, 181, 205, 207
Pir, 80
Piram, 154
Pir-napishtim, 80
Poebel, Arno, 78, 81, 106, 112, 137, 157, 173, 181
Pognon, H., 50, 64, 124, 145, 157, 162
Prince, J. D., 100
Pudi-El, 140

qamar, 170
Qenan, 65
Qideshu, 152
QI-MASH, 129
Qi-Mash-qi, 128

Rameses II, 99, 103
Ranke, Hermann, 54, 79, 90, 96, 106, 109, 110, 112, 113, 123, 127, 161, 173, 186, 193, 209
Reissner, J., 99, 113
Rim-Aku, 193
Rim-Anum, 89
Rim-Sin, 64, 111
Rogers, R. W., 22, 55, 71, 91
Rosellini, 29

Sabbath, 55, 60, 61
Sachau, Eduard, 204

Salem, 154
Samaria, 60
Samu-el, 102
Samson, 125
Sanchoniathan, 52
Sarah, 40
Sargon, 90, 97, 181
Sarpânitu, 57, 133, 136
Sarugi, 189
Sayce, A. H., 29, 37, 44, 46, 55, 63, 66, 76, 89, 125, 141, 146, 147, 151, 152, 161, 181
Scheil, P. V., 73, 80, 110, 182, 183, 184, 186, 188
Schrader, E., 80
Schumacher, 26
Sha-Addu, 127
shabattum, 56
shabath, 61
Sha-imeri-shu, 130
Shalmaneser II, 98
Sha-Mash, 79, 127
Shamash, 38, 78, 80, 81, 82, 100, 104, 107, 118, 123, 125
Shamash-li-me-ri, 106
Shamash-li-wi-ir, 106
Shamash-napishtim, 80
Sha-NITA-shu, 130
sha-pat-tum, 55
SHAR-GA-NI-LUGAL-URU, 181
Shargani-shar-âli, 131
Shar-Gani-sharri, 113, 182
Shar-la-ak, 186
Sharrapu, 116
Shar-ri-ish-ta-qal, 186
Sharukin, 194
Shi-mi-Til-la, 103
Shinar, 91
Shum-Malik, 134
Shumer, 13
Shuqamuna, 114
Shur-ki-Til-la, 103
Sidon, 98
Siduna, 152
Siegfried, C., 162
Sihon, 145, 154
Simanu, 104

Sin, 16, 145, 200
Sinai, 87
Sin-mâgir, 193
Sin-iddinam, 192
Sinuhe novel, 29
Sippar, 47, 98, 173
Sisera, 145
Ṣit, 80
Ṣit-napishtim, 80
Steuernagel, C., 26
Strassmaier, J. N., 14, 80, 102, 105, 159, 162, 168
Stube, R., 162
Subsalla, 97
Sumu-abum, 89
ṢUR, 101

Ta'annek, 24, 27, 37
Ta-i-Til-la, 103
tabah, 76
Tallqvist, K. L., 101, 127, 128, 133, 144
Talmud, 68
Tammuz, 16, 20
Tarkhu, 136
Tehom, 49, 50
Te-ḫi-ip-Til-la, 103
Tela, 103
Tell-Deilam, 170
Tell el-Amarna, 32, 38
Tell el-Mutesselim, 26
Terah, 168
Thureau-Dangin, F., 111, 115, 143, 180, 181, 182, 184, 187, 188
Ti'amat, 46, 48, 148
ti'amtu, 49, 50, 53
Tidanu, 97
Tidnu, 96, 102, 103
Tiele, C. P., 141, 181
Tiglathpileser I, 60, 98
Tilla, 102, 103
Tillah, 103
Til-Naḫiri, 172
Ti-ma-ash-gi, 129
Ti-mi-Til-la, 103
Ti-ra-mas-qi, 129
Toffteen, O. A., 98

Tripolis, 76
Tyre, 98

Ubar-Tutu, 66
U-bi-in-shar-ri, 185
UD, 80
UD-ḪUL-GAL, 58
UD-TU, 100
ummanu, 65
Um-napishtim, 80
Ungnad, Arthur, 81, 84, 86, 105, 106, 140, 145, 147, 170, 209
Ur, 16, 95
UR-A, 113
Urarṭu, 75
Urash, 89, 122
Ur-billum, 180
Ur dynasty, 96, 97
Ur-Engur, 192
Urfa, 103, 167, 170
Ur-ḫa-lu-ub, 120
Ûri, 13, 102, 192
Uri(or *Eri*)-*Aku*, 112
U-ri-gal-la, 115
Ur-karinnu, 120
Ur-Kasdim, 170
U-ri-Marduk, 117
Ur-NIN-IB, 118, 193
Ur-NIN-MAR, 199
Ur-Pad, 180
Urra, 109, 113, 114
Urra-bâni, 109
Urra-BA-TIL, 109
Urra-gal, 82, 115
urru, 105
Ursalimmu, 105, 175, 180
Urṭu, 102
Ûru, 38, 78, 109
Uru-Az, 180
Uru(URU)-BA-SAG-SAG, 112
URU-DINGIR-RA, 110
ÛRU-KA-GI-NA, 112, 113
Ûru(URU)-ki-bi, 112
URU-LIG-GA, 110
ÛRU-milki, 102, 105, 134
Urumma, 167
URU-MU, 110
Uru-MU-USH, 112

INDEX

Uru(URU)-NI-BA-AGA, 112
URU-RA, 110
U-ru-sa-lim, 152, 175
Urya, 107
USH, 110, 113
Ush-bi-Sah, 140
Ushpia, 140
UT, 80
U-ta-na-ish-tim, 81
Ut-napishtim, 67, 77, 80
U-tu-ki, 117
UTU-napishtim, 134

Vashti, 127
Vincent, 27
Viranshehir, 103

Ward, W. H., 28, 43, 57, 87, 88, 132, 135, 136
Warad-Sin, 110

Wellhausen, J., 128
Winckler, H., 14, 16, 17, 21, 68, 139

Xisuthrus, 64

Yahweh, 45, 51, 86, 87, 88, 89, 90
Yahweh-jireh, 178
Yahweh-nissi, 178
Yahweh-Sebaoth, 121
Yahweh-shalom, 178

Zakir, 64, 158
Zamama, 89
Zimmern, H., 17, 48, 56, 63, 64, 65, 72, 79, 80, 81, 89, 100, 114, 115, 131, 133, 134, 198, 199
Ziri-Bashani, 151

www.ingramcontent.com/pod-product-compliance
Lightning Source LLC
Chambersburg PA
CBHW071312110426
42743CB00042B/1321